Teacher Retention: What is Your Weakest Link?

India J. Podsen

EYE ON EDUCATION
6 DEPOT WAY WEST, SUITE 106
LARCHMONT, NY 10538
(914) 833–0551
(914) 833–0761 fax
www.eyeoneducation.com

Library of Congress Cataloging-in-Publication Data

Podsen, India, 1945-
     Teacher retention : what is your weakest link?/India J. Podsen.
          p. cm.
     Includes bibliographical references (p.).
     ISBN 1-930556-36-5
     1. Teacher turnover--United States--Prevention. 2. Teacher effectiveness--United States. 3. Teachers--In-service training--United States. I. Title.

LB2833.2 .P63 2002
371.14--dc21   2001059785

10 9 8 7 6 5 4 3 2 1

Editorial and production services provided by
Richard H. Adin Freelance Editorial Services
52 Oakwood Blvd., Poughkeepsie, NY 12603-4112
(845-471-3566)

Also Available from EYE ON EDUCATION

Coaching and Mentoring
First-Year and Student Teachers
India Podsen, and Vicki Denmark

Handbook on Teacher Portfolios
for Evaluation and Professional Development (Includes CD-ROM)
Pamela Tucker, James Stronge, and Christopher Gareis

Staff Development:
Practices That Promote Leadership in Learning Communities
Sally Zepeda

Human Resources Administration:
A School-Based Perspective 2/e
Richard E. Smith

Motivating and Inspiring Teachers:
The Educator's Guide for Building Staff Morale
Todd Whitaker, Beth Whitaker, and Dale Lumpa

Dealing with Difficult Teachers
Todd Whitaker

Teaching Matters
Motivating and Inspiring Yourself
Todd and Beth Whitaker

Feeling Great!
The Educator's Guide For Eating Better,
Exercising Smarter, and Feeling Your Best
Todd Whitaker and Jason Winkle

Dealing with Difficult Parents
Todd Whitaker and Douglas J. Fiore

Bouncing Back!
How Your School Can Succeed in the Face of Adversity
Jerry Patterson, Janice Patterson, and Loucrecia Collins

The Emerging Principalship
By Linda Skrla, David Erlandson, etc.

Introduction to Educational Leadership
and Organizational Behavior
Patti L. Chance and Edward W. Chance

Creating Connections for Better Schools:
How Leaders Enhance School Culture
Douglas J. Fiore

Geese, such as the ones pictured on the cover of this book, provide lessons for educators:

♦ As each goose flaps its wings, it creates an uplift for the birds that follow. By flying in "Y" formation, the whole flock adds 71% greater flying range than if each bird flew alone.

Lesson: People who share a common direction and sense of community can get where they are going quicker and easier, because they are traveling on the thrust of one another.

♦ When a goose falls out of formation, it suddenly feels the drag and resistance of flying alone, and quickly gets back into formation to take advantage of the "lifting power" of the bird immediate in front.

Lesson: If we have as much sense as a goose, we will stay in formation with those who are headed where we want to go and be willing to accept their help, as well as give ours to others.

♦ When the lead goose gets tired, it rotates back into the formation and another goose flies to the point position.

Lesson: It pays to take turns doing the hard tasks and sharing leadership. As with geese, people are interdependent on each other's skills, capabilities and unique arrangements of gifts, talents or resources.

♦ The geese flying in formation honk from behind to encourage those in front to keep up their speed.

Lesson: We need to make sure our honking is encouraging. In groups where there is encouragement the production is greater. The power of encouragement (to stand by one's heart or core values and encourage the heart and core of others) is the quality of honking we seek.

♦ When a goose gets sick, wounded, or shot down, two geese drop out of the formation and follow it down to help and protect it. They stay with it until it is able to fly again or dies. Then they launch out on their own, with another formation or catch up with the flock.

Lesson: If we have as much sense as geese, we too will stand by each other in difficult times as well as when we are strong.

Adapted from a speech given by Angeles Arrien
at the 1991 Organizational Developmental
Network, based on the work of Milton Olson.

Table of Contents

Acknowledgments

I am part of all that I have met.

Alfred Lord Tennyson

Becoming a *competent, caring, and committed teacher* doesn't just happen—it evolves from a myriad of human interactions, learning sources, conversations, and experiences. The quote above summarizes how I feel about both family members and professional colleagues who have had a significant influence on my life and the many educators and students with whom I have had the privilege to work with over the past 25 years.

I am proud to be associated with Dr. Robert Michael, Dean of the School of Education, and Dr. Susan Gannaway, Teacher Education Department Chair, and the faculty at North Georgia College & State University. They have done, and continue to do, an excellent job in preparing teachers for tomorrow's schools. I have learned what a true professional learning community can be, as I have worked with colleagues who are dedicated and talented teachers and faculty mentors.

In particular, I wish to express my thanks to the first three cohorts of teacher leaders who took on the unknown when they entered the newly designed Education Specialist Program in Teacher Leadership at NGCSU and the many school practitioners who worked diligently to make this effort a true partnership among all stakeholders. The work of these teacher leaders in their schools and in this program has been awesome. Being a part of their journey as they wrestled with school-based problems and their own professional growth, led to the development of this book. Hopefully, the ideas expressed in this book will initiate conversations about ways teachers can take a proactive role in reaching their full potential as educators.

A special thanks goes to Carolyn Clarke, principal, friend, and colleague, who keeps me grounded in the real world of teaching and learning.

India Podsen
March 2002

I

Sizing Up the Situation

1

Teacher Shortages: A Profession at Risk

Are teacher shortages an area of concern or perhaps a serious problem in your school or school district? Does your school system Web page look like the one below that we pulled off the Internet for a large urban school system? Are you starting each school year with an increasing number of teacher vacancies? Are you losing your beginning teachers within the first 1 to 3 years of job entry? Do you feel your veteran teachers are marking time until retirement? Do you know why?

2001–2002 Teacher Shortages

The following certification areas have been found to be among the teaching shortages in our school district:

Shortages

all special education areas	speech clinicians
library science (media specialists)	science (all areas)
business education	industrial technology
mathematics	art
English/language arts	elementary education
family and consumer science (home economics)	foreign language (Spanish, French and Latin)
early childhood	

Teaching-force demographics show that one-third of the nation's teachers have more than 20 years of experience and two-thirds are at least at mid-career (Promising Practices, 1998). Concurrently, K–12 enrollment is at its highest, and projected enrollments are stretching the capacity of many schools. Schools already struggling to recruit competent teachers face serious shortages, especially in critical needs areas such as math, science, and special education.

Over two million new K–12 teachers will be employed in the United States over the next decade as a result of increased student enrollments, reductions in class size, and accelerating retirements among an aging teacher population (Darling-Hammond, 1997). More than one-third of these teachers will be hired in urban and rural school districts, and the majority of inner-city public schools will contain minority enrollments. However, the gap between the diversity of students in schools and the racial and ethnic characteristics of the teaching force is another recruitment issue challenging the nation's schools. "About 86 percent of the teachers in public schools are non-Hispanic Caucasian, while more than 32 percent of the students in K-12 schools are minority. This gap is growing larger" (Promising Practices, 1998, p. 1). The emerging population of new teachers will be challenged to educate a growing number of diverse learners in an increasingly complex technological society. Santrock (2001) tells us that effective teachers need to be brokers "between the culture of the school and the culture of certain students, especially those who are unsuccessful academically" (p.13).

As a teacher educator, school administrator, and teacher leader, what steps have you taken to ensure the successful transition of the novice from pre-service experiences into the real-world job realities of full-time teaching? Furthermore, how do you involve your teaching staff in this endeavor and why is their participation critical? As a staff developer, school principal, and classroom teacher, what are you willing to do differently to make sure the next generation of teachers gets a far better start than you did?

If you are wrestling with these questions, you are not alone. The literature on teacher retention tells us that more than 20 percent of public school teachers leave their positions within three years of employment and almost 10 percent quit before finishing their first year (Recruiting New Teachers, Inc. 1999). Unfortunately, our first-year teachers are often left to figure it out on their own with a professional development approach that has outlived its usefulness and little systematic support from colleagues (Lieberman, 2000).

Furthermore, well-organized and implemented induction programs are the exception, rather than the trend, and hit-and-miss induction experiences have been associated with higher levels of teacher attrition as well as lower levels of teacher effectiveness (National Commission on Teaching America's Future, 1996). The questions that loom before us are these:

- ♦ Are we primed to do things differently to develop the talent and skills of those entering our profession? If yes, what is our primary motivation?

- ♦ Are we willing to critically examine induction approaches that manage to attract qualified candidates but fail to keep them in the profession or worse provide a survival mentality?

♦ Are we prepared to seize the day to really look at what we do in our training programs and schools to support teacher learning and professional development?

♦ Are we ready as a dedicated community to design a career induction program that begins the process of professional learning and promotes a vision of professional development for a lifetime of practice?

Status of Teaching: The Big Picture

Based on data from the American Association of Colleges for Teacher Education (AACTE) Education Policy Clearinghouse (Laitsch, 2001), policy makers in more than 20 states have taken legislative action around the issues of teacher quality and teacher shortages. Most consistent is the support for National Board for Professional Teacher Standards (NBPTS) and teacher recruitment programs. Many new policies are showing a renewed effort by states to deal with issues of quality and supply in innovative approaches. Here are a few examples:

♦ **Shortages Issues**

  • Extension of scholarship and loan forgiveness programs

  • Increased support for NBPTS certification

  • Giving reciprocity for national board certification

♦ **Teacher Quality Issues**

  • Draft resolutions to examine areas for future legislative activity, including issues related to: (a) uncertified pubic school employees; (b) the impact on candidate ethnicity, gender, socioeconomic status, and age of using Pre-Professional Skills Test for admission into teacher preparation programs; and (c) the demand for, and preparation of, classroom teachers as well as determining the adequacy of pre-service and in-service training.

♦ **Professional Development Issues**

  • Assessment of teacher preparation programs.

  • Enactment of 1 to 3 year mentorship/induction programs.

  • Ability of community colleges to provide coursework in K–12 education and professional development.

  • Establishment of alternate certification programs for degreed individuals or certification as an educational assistant.

- Allowing distance-learning methods to account for 50 percent of continuing education requirements.

♦ **Certification Issues**

- Use of uncertified or out-of-field teachers in a classroom is limited to 30 days unless a waiver is obtained by the state board of education, which requires written notification to parents of affected students.

- Teachers with at least 30 years of experience are granted a lifetime license.

♦ **Testing Issues**

- Exemption of teachers who have previous experience from licensure exams.

- Postponement of Praxis II subject area exams for up to one year.

♦ **Whole System Reform**

Adoption of a more systematic approach to broad teacher quality reforms that focus on:

- induction and mentoring

- professional development and best practices

- additional team-based variable pay compensation when student performance improves

- implementation of a comprehensive continuum of data-driven strategies concerning recruitment, pre-service, licensure, induction, professional development and evaluation.

(Adapted and paraphrased from AACTE Legislative Update—
www. edpolicy.org)

The National Commission on Teaching and America's Future (1996), after conducting research over the last 10 years, concluded that "the single most important factor influencing student learning is *teacher expertise*, measured by teacher experience and master's degrees as well as *teacher performance* on statewide teacher examinations." One study, in particular, found that funds spent on qualified teachers resulted in greater improvements in student performance than any other allocation of school resources. Highlights of their findings indicated:

♦ Hiring and recruiting practices are not in line with current standards.

♦ School districts lack systems and resources to attract and retain qualified candidates.

♦ Professional development offerings do not meet the demands created by new standards for student learning.

♦ School systems do not have formulas to reward expert teaching performance.

The Commission concluded that "we know what to do in order to connect teacher learning to student learning—there is just no state or school system that has put together all the pieces of the teacher development continuum (i.e., recruitment, selection, preparation, evaluation, professional development, and reward).

Teacher Retention—A Pressing Problem

Concerns about teachers and teaching seem to reoccur whenever teacher supply and demand problems raise their threatening alarm. As a result, there are the predicable responses, such as catch-up salary increases, bonuses for early contract signing, new scholarship programs for prospective teachers, additional professional development dollars, and more focus on teacher induction and support programs.

When supply and demand problems ebb, however, there is the tendency to slip back to business as usual, and little, if anything, changes. Teacher pay continues to lag behind in many school districts, college preparation programs go on as before, and professional development activities, for the vast majority of teachers, remain random and unconnected to substantial school reform. As the ranks continue to dwindle, unqualified teachers are embraced into the classroom under quick-fix programs, which continue to reinforce the notion that anybody can teach.

The purpose of this guide is to raise questions about the problems and risk factors that affect teacher recruitment and retention and to suggest ways for school practitioners to address these issues within their schools in collaboration with faculty and staff. We firmly believe that the majority of teachers are strongly motivated to increase their knowledge and skill in the classroom because they truly want to make a difference. The focus of school-based improvement teams is to figure out pathways to release the intellectual and leadership capacity of all teachers: pathways that motivate teachers to actively seek and set professional goals that meet both their career interests and the needs of the school community. We do not want to imply that we have any hard and fast answers to these problems. We do want to assist you by providing additional information and insight that may be useful in your quest to attract and retain talented teachers in your school.

Teacher Development—Stagnant or Dynamic?

According to humanistic psychologist Abraham Maslow (2001), individuals strive for self-actualization and share a desire to acquire knowledge, be creative, and reach their full potential. We think educators are the best examples of this statement. "Education is about learning how to deal with uncertainty and ambiguity. It is about learning how to savor the journey. It is about inquiry and deliberation. It is about becoming critically-minded and intellectually curious, and it is about learning how to frame and pursue your own educational aims" (Novick, 1996, p.1; Eisner, 1992).

We enter our profession as a beginning teacher full of enthusiasm and sense of wonder. We have the desire to save the world and be the best teacher there ever was. "And we know how crushing it is to realize that's not going to happen—at least not for the first year" (Humphrey, 2000). As experienced teachers, we strive to grow professionally. We seek out graduate programs and attend required staff development programs to improve our practice, keep our certification current, and address current reform efforts. Yet, it seems the more we are required to do to get our students ahead, the further we get behind.

As the job settles into predictable routines, we find ourselves wondering, "*Is this all there is?*" We begin to think more of retirement and, perhaps, of moving to a new career as our morale, which once was high, fades with each passing year. We look back and ponder what happened to our passion and sense of mission to make schools a better place for teaching and learning.

How many experienced teachers come to school each day and go through the motions of teaching while watching the clock inch closer to the magic year of retirement? How many beginning teachers end their journey abruptly, leaving the profession within the first five years, feeling disillusioned and unsuccessful? What can we do about it? Why do we need to do something about it?

Teacher Workplaces—Friend or Foe?

Examining factors related to the teachers' workplace, Rosenholtz (1989) asserted that when teachers felt supported in their efforts of teaching and learning, they were more effective than those teachers who did not receive this type of affirmation. Teachers with a high sense of self-actualization were more likely to examine and experiment with innovative classroom behaviors and more likely to remain in the profession. Similarly, McLaughlin and Talbert (1993) concluded that teachers engaging in collaborative inquiry and learning resulting from that effort were able to develop and share a body of knowledge derived from their practice. "Support by means of teacher networks, cooperation among colleagues, and expanded professional roles increased teacher efficacy in meeting students' needs" (Hord, 2001, p. 2).

When teacher morale is high, students typically show higher levels of achievement, but, when teacher morale sinks, achievement levels decline and other problems come to the surface. "Low teacher morale can lead to indifference toward others, cynical attitudes toward students, little initiative when it comes to teaching and participating in school activities, preoccupation with leaving teaching for a better job, increased sick leave, and episodes of depression" (Black, 2001, p. 40). A 1996 study of a Texas public school system found that 44 percent of the teachers surveyed were seriously considering leaving the profession and at least one-third of these teacher cited "poor working conditions" as a major reason (Black, 2001). Comments from teachers in the study identified the following reasons as contributing to low teacher morale:

- ◆ A bureaucratic jungle
- ◆ Out-of-pocket expenses for classroom materials
- ◆ Long hours of lesson preparation and grading papers
- ◆ Unsafe schools and unruly students
- ◆ Menial duties and chores
- ◆ Weak and rigid curriculum
- ◆ Ineffective school policies
- ◆ Too much paperwork and testing
- ◆ Left out of the information loop

Two researchers (Black 2001) who conducted an international review of 67 studies on teacher stress summarized their findings in the following list of factors that contribute to low job satisfaction worldwide:

- ◆ Time constraints
- ◆ Excessive workload
- ◆ Low salaries
- ◆ Insufficient resources
- ◆ Large classes
- ◆ Lack of involvement in decision making
- ◆ Lack of collegiality and a sense of school community
- ◆ Problems with student discipline
- ◆ Few opportunities for promotions and advancements

Black (2001) concludes that teachers tend to be motivated more by intrinsic rewards such as self-respect, responsibility, and a sense of accomplishment than by extrinsic rewards. Teachers measure their job satisfaction by such factors as participating in decision making, using their skills in ways that are valued, having freedom and independence, being challenged, expressing their creativity and having opportunities to learn. Recent studies indicate that there is not a lack of teachers to fill the needed vacancies but rather that teachers view conditions in the workplace as either overwhelming or intolerable. What are we doing to keep the workplace user-friendly?

The Leadership Factor

Schools that show sustained levels of success with students also show consistent profiles of work environments that facilitate and value a strong sense of professional community (Little, 1996). The term professional community can be defined as a learning community in which teachers and administrators continuously seek and share learning, and then act on what they learn (Asuto et. al, 1993). The goal of their actions is to enhance their effectiveness as professionals so that students benefit. These learning communities:

- Inquire into student learning and achievement a central focus for both individual teachers and as a group.

- Organize physical space, time, and resources in ways that reduce professional isolation and embed opportunities for teacher learning and development from within and outside the classroom.

- Use professional development resources to increase the school's ability to acquire feedback on its performance, evaluate emerging trends and needs, and make informed decisions about new ideas, materials, and colleagues (Little, 1996).

Macmillan (1999) proposes that traditional, rigid, bureaucratically administered schools result in low teacher commitment and job satisfaction whereas progressive and flexible schools that use collaborative problem-solving strategies promote a feeling of affiliation with the school and raise teacher satisfaction. He concludes that in more flexible schools, teachers believe they can contribute to positive school-wide changes and that their contributions will be sought after and valued. Black (2001) surmises that when it comes to teacher morale, it all comes down to school leadership and the principal. School leaders who value and strive to implement the characteristics of professional learning communities have significant positive impact on teacher performance and retention (Vernadine, 1997).

A Proposal

So what does this all mean for you sitting in the trenches dealing with teacher shortages and losing the ones you finally managed to find? We know there are no quick fixes and even less time to deal with rising accountability reforms, teaching and learning issues, personnel problems, and a myriad of other duties and responsibilities. In collaboration with school practitioners at both building and central office levels, and aspiring teacher leaders involved in an Educational Specialist Program in Teacher Leadership at North Georgia College & State University (NGCSU), we have examined the risk factors they face in the workplace and brainstormed approaches about how to address the problem of retaining not only beginning teachers but also experienced, competent teachers. The journal entries interspersed throughout the text are the voices of these teacher leaders and school practitioners involved in this new degree program at NGCSU. The names have been changed to ensure confidentiality.

We believe the issue of teacher retention is a symptom of a larger more deep seated belief system about the work culture of schools that needs to be restructured (Glickman, 2001). Current school reform efforts are urging us to develop and initiate not only new notions of teaching and learning to support student achievement but also a wide variety of practices that support teacher learning and career growth (Lieberman, 2000; Santrock, 2001).

We are particularly concerned with teacher self-efficacy and its impact on teacher retention. Perceived self-efficacy is defined as a person's judgments of one's capabilities to organize and execute courses of action to attain desired goals. Zimmerman (2001) asserts that "self-efficacy beliefs provide learners with a sense of agency to motivate their learning through use of such self-regulatory processes as goal-setting, self-monitoring, self-evaluation, and strategy use. Consequently, the more capable learners judge themselves to be, the more challenging the goals they take on" (p. 156).

A survey of teacher attitudes across the nation indicates that approximately 26 percent of teachers think it's a waste of their time to try to do their best, and 15 percent plan to leave as soon as possible (National Center for Education Statistics for the U.S. Department of Education, 1993–94). Teacher attitudes about their ability to make a difference in the classroom play an important role in their decision to remain in the profession.

Conclusion

This book is intended to help teacher-preparation educators, building-level leaders, staff developers, and teacher mentors address school-work patterns in five critical areas assembled from the professional literature that may impact teacher attrition and retention. In addition, the book supports a view of professional development that fosters the active involvement of teachers in customizing their own professional development action plans that are based on explicit career stages. These stages are guided by national standards and benchmarks to challenge teachers to aspire to expert levels within their content area and school community.

"Effective teachers develop a positive identity, seek advice from experienced teachers, maintain their own learning, and build up good resources and supports" (Santrock, 2001, p. 15). We also hope the career framework provides a systematic structure for school districts and schools to assist in organizing their professional development resources and finding ways to reward and recognize truly talented teachers. The ultimate goal is teacher self-actualization, which in turn promotes confidence building and teacher efficacy.

What we present is a summary of our conversations as we have struggled to (a) prepare new teachers and watch them falter during their first years even after close mentoring; and (b) rejuvenate experienced teachers who show signs of early burnout and potential career withdrawal. Many of our ideas will need to be tested in the field. Hopefully, our suggestions will stimulate thought and a call to action on the shared goal of developing and keeping enthusiastic and competent teachers in our classrooms.

References

Adams, R. D., & Martray, C. (1981, April). *Teacher development: A study of factors related to teacher concerns for pre-beginning, and experienced teachers.* Paper presented at annual meeting of the American Educational Research Association, Los Angeles.

Astuto, T. A., Clark, D. L., Rend, A. M., McGree, K., & Fernandez, L.P. (1993). *Challenges to dominant assumptions controlling educational reform.* Andover, MA: Regional Laboratory for the Educational Improvement of the Northwest and Islands.

Black, S. (2001, January). Morale matters. *American School Board Journal,* 40–43.

Darling-Hammond, L. (1997). *Doing what matters most: Investing in quality teaching.* New York: National Commission on Teaching & America's Future.

Eisner, E. W. (1991). What really counts in schools. *Educational Leadership, 48*(5), 10–17.

Ethell, R., & McMeniman, M. M. (2001, March–April). Unlocking the knowledge in action of an expert practitioner. *Journal of Teacher Education, 51*(2), 87–101.

Glickman, C., Gordon, S., & Ross-Gordon, J. (2001). *SuperVision and instructional leadership.* Boston, MA: Allyn and Bacon.

Gold, Y. (1996). Beginning teacher support. Attrition, mentoring, and induction. In C. B. Courtney (Ed.), *Review of Research in Education*, 16, (pp. 548–594). Washington, DC: American Educational Research Association.

Hord, S. (1997). Professional learning communities: What they are and why they are important.. *Issues About Change,* Austin, TX: Southwest Educational Development Lab, 6(1).

Humphrey, T. (2001, August/September). Knowing enough for now. *Reading Today*, 4.

Laitsch, D. (2001). Legislative update. *AACTE Education Policy Clearinghouse* 1(1). http://www.edpolicy.org. Retrieved 11/10/01.

Lieberman, A. (2000). *Practices that support teacher development: Transforming conceptions of professional learning.* htttp://www.her.nsf.gov/HER/REC/pubs/NSF_EF/lieber.htm). Retrieved 11/17/00.

Little, J. W. (1996). *Excellence in professional development and professional community.* National Specialty in School Change: Key Issues: Selected Readings About Student Learning. http://www.org/scpd/natspecl/excellecne.html. Retrieved 2/15/01.

Macmillan, R. (1999, September). Influences of workplace conditions on teachers' job satisfaction. *The Journal of Educational Research,* 39.

Maslow, A. (2001). Self-actualizing people: A study of psychological health. In R. Diessner & J. Tiegs (Eds.), *Human Development* (pp. 307–315). Guilford, CT: McGraw Hill/Dushkin.

McLaughlin, M. W., & Talbert, J. E. (1993). *Contexts that matter for teaching and learning.* Stanford, CA: Center for Research on the Context of Secondary School Teaching, Stanford University.

Meier, D. (1992, Summer). Reinventing teaching. *Teachers College Record*, 93(4), 594–609.

Mesiter, D. G., & Jenks, C. (2000, March–April). Making the transition from preservice to inservice: Beginning teachers reflections. *Journal of the Association of Teacher Education, 51*(2), 87–101.

National Commission on Teaching & America's Future. (1996). *What matters most: Teaching for America's Future.* New York: Author, Teachers College, Columbia University.

National Center for Education Statistics for the U.S. Department of Education (1993–94). Schools and Staffing Survey. In *Teacher Teaching in the Southeast: A Special Columbia Group Report, 1997,* Raleigh, NC: Koger Center.

Novick, R. (1996). Actual schools, possible practices: New directions in professional development. *Education Policy Analysis Archives* 4(14). Available from: http://epaa.asu.edu/epaa/v4n14.html

Recruiting New Teachers, Inc. (1999). *Learning the ropes: Urban teacher induction programs and practices in the United States.* Belmont, MA.

Rosenholtz, S. (1989). *Teachers' workplace: The social organization of schools.* New York: Longman.

Santrock, J. (2001). *Educational psychology.* New York, NY: McGraw-Hill Higher Education.

Steffey, B. E., Wolfe, M. P., Pasch, S. H., & Enz, B. J. (Eds.). (2000). *Life cycle of the career teacher.* Thousand Oaks, CA: Corwin Press.

U.S. Department of Education. (1998). *Promising practices: Recruiting talented and diverse people into the teaching profession.* Washington, DC: Available from: http://www.ed.gov/pubs/PromPractice/chapter2.html

Vernadine, T. (1997). *What research says about administrators' management style, effectiveness, and teacher morale.* ERIC Document ED411569.

Zimmerman, B. J. (2000). Self-efficacy: An essential motive to learn. In *Educational Psychology Annual Edition* (2001–2002 ed., pp. 156–159). Guilford, CT: McGraw–Hill/Dushkin.

2

Career Staging: A Professional Framework

Using What We Know

Daniel Levinson (2001) in *A Conception of Adult Development* tells us that there is little theory, research, or cultural wisdom about the series of age levels after adolescence. Words such as *youth, maturity,* and *middle age* are ambiguous in their age linkages and meanings. He asserts that "the ambiguity of language stems from the lack of any cultural definition of adulthood and how people's lives evolve within it" (p. 299). He concludes that "we have a detailed picture of many trees but no view of the forest and no map to guide our journey through it."

Likewise, we have well over three million teachers, but no history of a defined career progression within the teaching profession. Generally, new teachers and experienced teachers are given similar assignments, assessed by the same evaluation standards, and expected to carry the same workloads. Pay raises are the same for all teachers within the employed system and there are few incentives or rewards that foster authentic professional development.

Teacher satisfaction surveys clearly show that one of the factors affecting long-term teacher retention is the lack of opportunities for promotions and advancement (Black, 2001). In addition, the current professional literature tells us that our teacher preparation and development programs show no systematic linkages to how adults evolve within the profession, particularly as it relates to adult learning and life span transitions (Gehrke, 1991). Without a staged career path, we too have no view of the forest, and, therefore, no map to guide us through it.

Adult Life Cycle Development

Levinson (2001) conceives of adult development as a sequence of eras. Each era has its own unique characteristics, and each makes a distinct contribution to the whole. There are major changes in the nature of adult lives from one era to the next, and minor, but still important, changes in the transition years between eras. A new era begins as the previous one is approaching its end. The eras and the overlapping transitions provide an underlying order in the flow of all adult lives, yet accommodate a wide array of variations in the individual life paths.

Each era and developmental period begins and ends at a well-defined modal age, with a range of about two years above and below this average. The idea of age-linked phases in adult life goes against conventional wisdom according to Levinson, but he contends that these age findings have been consistently verified in the research. Figure 2.1 summarizes these eras according to Levinson.

Patterns in Adult Learning

Research shows that adults do not learn in the same way as children (Cantor, 1992; Cranton, 1992). According to Stroot, et al., (1998) teaching adults requires the utilization of a process model rather than a content approach. The content model relies on a teacher-directed format in which the instructor usually determines what knowledge and skills need to be acquired. Conversely, the process model relies on a collaborative approach in which the learners acquire the necessary resources to obtain information and skills that meet their individual needs.

Adults, like children, vary in how they acquire knowledge. No one theory or approach can effectively meet the diverse needs, experiences, and cultures that adults bring to the learning context. However, critical study of adult learning can provide additional insight into the complex nature of adult training and development. Malcolm Knowles' (1994) theory of andragogy (adult learning) is an attempt to differentiate the ways adults learn from the way children learn. Stroot, et al., (1998) provide the outline presented in Figure 2.2 as a way to summarize the ideas of Knowles on this issue.

Figure 2.1. Eras of Adulthood

ERAs	Age Range	Key Characteristics
Preadult-hood	Birth to age 22	• Moves from highly dependent states—infancy—childhood—adolescence—to a more independent adult life • Era of rapid physical, social, and psychological growth
Early Adult Transition	Age 17 to 22	• Modification of relationships with parents and family • Developmental bridge where the early adult reappraises the existing structure and makes choices for a new structure.
Early Adulthood	Age 22 to 40	• Era of greatest energy, abundance, contradiction and stress. • The 20s and 30s are peak years biologically • Era for forming and pursuing youthful dreams, establishing a niche, raising a family • A time for status and recognition and occupational advancement
Midlife Transition	Age 40 to 45	• Termination of early adulthood and the start of middle adulthood • Key developmental task is the process of individuation. The adult becomes more compassionate, more reflective, more judicious, less ruled by inner conflicts and external demands
Middle Adulthood	Age 40 to 65	• Biological capabilities begin to decline • Senior status in unique worlds and the desire to be responsible not only for own work but also for the development of the current generation of young adults who will soon follow
Late Adulthood	Age 60 to 65	• Thoughtful confrontation • Concerns about health rise • Career retirement

Figure 2.2. Comparison Between Children and Adult Learning Characteristics

Assumptions	Children	Adults
Learner's Concept	Dependent	Independent—Self-directed
Learner's Experience	Limited in resource learning	Rich in resource learning
Learner's Readiness	Based on physical, mental, and social development	Based on need
Relevancy	Later application	Immediate application
Curriculum	Subject-centered, teacher-directed	Problem-centered, collaborative, informal, respective to job
Planning	By the teacher	Mutual between facilitator and adult
Determination of Needs	By the teacher	Mutual and self-diagnosis
Lesson Design	Sequenced in terms of subject matter, content-focused	Sequenced in terms of needs, problem-focused
Activities	Transmittal of information and skills	Experiential techniques, realistic and authentic to what is required on the job
Evaluation	By the teacher	Mutual with self-monitoring and action planning follow-up

The principles of adult learning can provide a framework for analyzing the development of teachers as they become expert practitioners. A synthesis of research findings (Peredo, 2001) indicates that there are basically four major adult learning principles:

1. **Adults are self-directing and desire to be in charge of their learning, including the content, time, and effort**. Adults learn better if there is a component of self-direction in the design of induction, mentoring, and corresponding professional development programs. Adults prefer flexible schedules that respond to their own time constraints, and they learn better when the learning is individualized. This factor may have important implications in designing professional development programs for teachers who often complain that most staff development programs do not meet their needs. Adult learners seem to learn better if there is an atmosphere

of mutual assistance, peer support, and collegial trust and acceptance. They value teaching strategies that increase their autonomy and value their thoughts and ideas.

2. **Adults' prior life experiences play a key role in their learning activities, and they rely on these experiences as a resource from which they can learn new things.** This factor may be especially important in the induction of alternate certification teachers coming from other careers. Both teacher preparation and local staff development programs may need to incorporate more experiential training activities in order build for transfer of prior knowledge and skills applicable to the classroom. Adult learners derive the greatest benefit from instructional methods that assist them in processing their experiences through reflection, analysis, and critical examination. They seem to benefit from active participation in the learning process.

3. **Adults have distinctive learning styles, with their routines and strategies for processing information already established.** Adults tend to be problem-centered and want to see the link between what they are learning and problems they are experiencing on the job. Adult learners value cooperative learning and are motivated by practical, how-to learning approaches. Cantor (1992) tells us that adults seek to: (a) make or maintain social relationships, (b) meet performance expectations, (c) learn to better serve others, (d) achieve personal and professional advancement, and (e) pursue intellectual stimulation and interest.

4. **Adults pass through various developmental stages, and this impacts the type and methods of learning in which they will engage.** Adult learning may be more effective if it takes into consideration differences in adult life span development, career stages, interests, and specific occupational tasks of the assigned position. Adults have accumulated life experiences and tend to learn more readily when peer coaches/instructors adopt a role of facilitator rather then lecturer or evaluator.

Barriers to Adult Learning

Because adults have accumulated life experiences, they also have unique problems that may impact on their ability to immerse themselves in learning activities. Cantor (1992) gives us these points to consider about potential barriers:

♦ Concurrent role responsibilities (family, career, social, political commitments)

♦ Lack of time and/or money

+ Lack of child care

+ Scheduling problems

+ Transportation problems

+ Insufficient confidence

+ Having to learn, if mandated, but not interested or ready

Teacher Development

According to Peredo (2001), teachers begin to acquire knowledge and skill particular to their profession by linking theory or technical knowledge learned in pre-service or staff development settings to practical or procedural knowledge learned in the daily practice of teaching. The learning curve is accelerated through practical application gained from dealing with real-life classroom situations rather than further formal instruction. Teachers, according to Peredo, tend to learn the most in specific situations that call for decision making and ownership for actions. The challenge for both pre-service and in-service education is to find ways to build upon these highly specific experiences so learning is transferred to other teachers and across situations.

Nearly every state in the nation is involved in the movement to raise academic standards. This movement is requiring higher standards in the practice of teaching (CPRE Policy Brief, 1995) and the shift from a behaviorist approach to teaching (teacher-generated knowledge and drill and practice) to approaches that actively engage students in the construction of knowledge and application of skills. This shift requires teachers to (a) possess in-depth perceptions of their subject matter and how it should be presented, (b) make choices about what content is essential, and (c) decide what assessments are needed to capture students' achievement. A key technique to help teachers build their knowledge and skill is reflective practice. Reflective practice requires teachers to review the decisions made in teaching a particular lesson or dealing with a current problem and then to explain the rationale for the decisions made. This process asks the teacher to question assumptions about his or her knowledge and skill base and link decisions to current best practices and classroom-based standards.

Because teachers are highly autonomous learners, they need to be actively involved in assessing their teaching performance based on classroom-based standards, setting learning goals, monitoring their progress, and collecting data to support their accomplishments. Teachers learn a great deal from both formal and informal interaction with others in their field. Such interaction may be through mentoring, peer coaching, conferences, networking, and professional development inquiry groups. To be successful, therefore, professional development programs for teachers must support such information interaction and build communities of learning.

Teaching is an information intensive endeavor and the integration of the knowledge and skills of all teachers in the school community provides a rich resource base for ongoing professional growth. If teachers are to be adequately prepared to work effectively in today's classrooms and schools, more effective approaches to professional development need to be envisioned. "Teachers and policy makers need to abandon long-held conventions about continuing education for teachers and begin to view professional development as an essential and integral part of teachers' work" (CPRE Policy Brief, 1995).

Career Staging: The Professional Educator Career Framework

Kay Awalt Musgrove, President of the Association for Supervision and Curriculum Development (Allen, 2001, p. 3), asserts that "the most important person in education is the classroom teacher. Everything needs to revolve around the teachers so they can get the job done." But, she adds, "teachers need to move out of their *comfort zones* and take *bold steps* to meet the needs of all children, especially in light of, or in spite of, the current climate of accountability."

What does stepping out of one's comfort zone mean? For this conversation, it means a continual and systematic effort to reassess one's professional life and where one is in that life. It means asking questions such as: "What is my teaching like now? What have I accomplished? Where do I spend most of my time and energy? What would make my professional life more satisfying or meaningful? Where am I in my career? Are there interests and needs which I would like to explore more fully?" Reflection on these questions, and others that emerge, help the teacher identify those aspects of the teaching career that have the greatest significance.

To help teachers answer these questions, we feel a career-staging framework should accomplish two objectives. First, it must meet the adult's developmental needs and characteristics for a specific, age-related time frame; and, second, it must meet the needs of our profession to promote competent, committed, and caring educators.

The career-staging framework provides a career path for teachers to use as a way to guide their own professional development. *Guide* is the key word. Based on what we know about adult learning and development, teachers need take a very active role in their own professional development at each career stage. The role of teacher preparation educators, school leaders, and staff developers is to promote, support, and facilitate teacher development within these stages. Teachers can no longer remain in a passive role, expecting school systems to meet their individual needs. However, school systems can no longer use a one-size-fits-all professional development model, if they truly aspire to help all teachers reach high levels of productivity. (Lieberman, 2000)

As a product of our review of the literature, observations of teachers, and an analysis of career paths of highly effective educators, we propose the Professional Educator Career Framework. The framework consists of four career stages, as shown in Figure 2.3, that could challenge classroom teachers to higher levels of competence, self-efficacy, and expansion into other professional roles. More important, we hope the framework will assist both teachers and school systems to begin a systematic journey to continuous school improvement.

Figure 2.3 The Professional Educator Career Framework

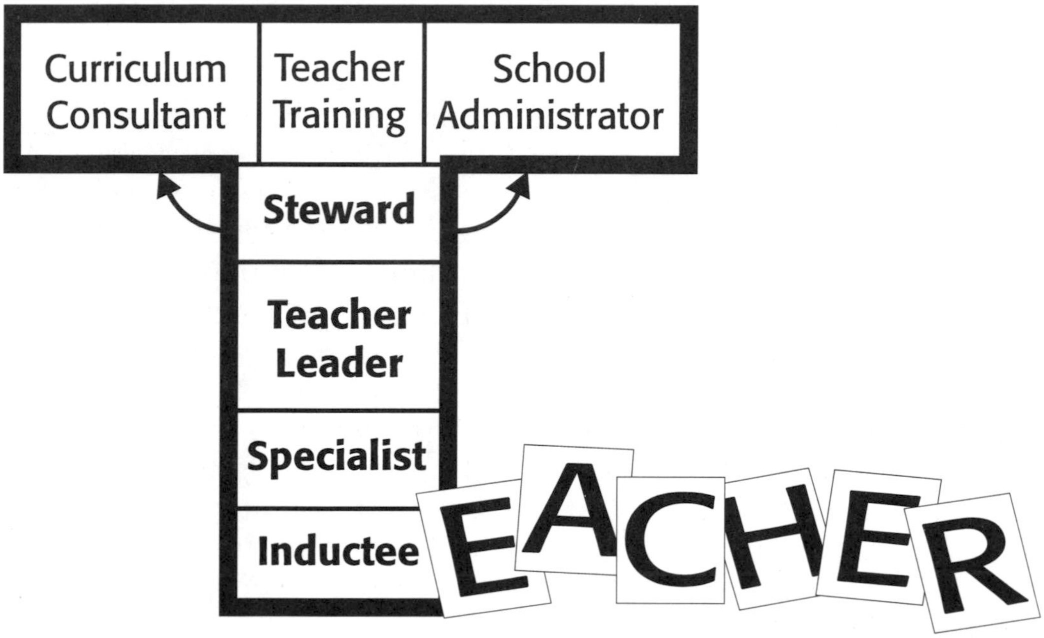

Teacher Inductee

Traditional Profile

This career stage begins for new teachers when they receive responsibility for planning and delivering instruction on their own. According to Steffey et al. (2000), "this phase continues until integration and synthesis of knowledge, pedagogy, and confidence emerges" and usually can last up to three years. Generally, the typical age range is between 21 to 24; however, alternate certification programs have changed the profile of the typical entry age. Teachers during this time in their lives are highly idealistic and filled with high expectations for themselves and their students. They seek formal acceptance into the profession and want to be valued as a teacher. Teachers new to the profession are focused on survival (Adams & Murray, 1981). They are concerned about doing well when a supervisor is observing, getting favorable evaluations, and being accepted and respected by students and other teachers.

Transferring what they have learned in their preparation program may be more of a challenge than they realized it would be. At this stage, new teachers often have sufficient knowledge and skill derived from clinical practicums and student teaching, but often show problems in applying these behaviors when the classroom content differs significantly from their pre-service experiences (Mesiter & Jenks, 2000). Studies of pre-service teachers indicate that they may need more exposure to expert teachers' cognitive reasoning processes through think-aloud interventions (Ethell & McMeniman, 2000).

Nontraditional Profile

For alternative-certification teachers, the typical age of their first year in teaching could range from 30 to 50. Induction approaches for adults transferring in from other professions and careers present an interesting challenge for teacher preparation faculty, school leaders, and staff developers. As the enormity of teacher shortages becomes a reality to many state policy makers and school systems, the need for greater flexibility in practices of hiring noncertified personnel has become a critical concern. In order to retain the valuable contribution of alternate-route teachers, more recent initiatives have focused on better recruitment policies and more structured preparation for classroom teaching, as well as skillful supervision and systematic support.

If we accept the four major principles of adult learning presented earlier, we may need to consider different options for selecting and training these individuals. First, we may want to conduct intensive interviews/surveys that seek data about the nature of the previous career, particularly as it relates to time management, interpersonal skills, leadership and management skills. In particular, assessing candidates' dispositions and attitudes about education, teaching, and learning would be critical in determining a best fit between those attributes needed for teaching and those that could prevent a successful transition. These profiles may help identify potential risk factors, attitudes, and gaps in essential knowledge and skills required for teaching in today's context.

Most adults have acquired a wide array of job related skills and the role of the induction process may need to include ways to identify previous knowledge and skill, and link that information to teaching. If prior life experiences do play a key role in learning for adults, then valuing these experiences and linking them to current teaching standards may help validate prior skills and experiences. Second, adults in this age group may respond better to induction approaches where the support teacher/instructor provides a more learner-centered approach and serves as a facilitator among equals, rather than a teacher-directed approach.

Training and support groups for alternative certification teachers may need to center more on problem-based learning rather than on theory-based teacher directed instruction. Case study method and micro-teaching analyses and reflections would capitalize on prior knowledge and skills. These would help alternative-certification teachers to critically reflect on how teaching and learning differs from the model they experienced as student learners, begin to challenge outdated perceptions, and seek more research-based approaches. Santrock (2001) cautions us that although a great deal of knowledge comes from personal experience, teachers need to check the validity of those truths and keep themselves grounded in current research findings and standards about teaching and learning.

An example of a program that seems to model many of the adult learning principles mentioned earlier is Project Promise, an alternate-certification program at Colorado State University (Promising Practices, 1998). This program attracts more than 300 degreed applicants each year from such fields as law, engineering, medicine, and government service. One-third of the applicants usually have a master's degree or first professional degree. Here is an outline of this program:

- *Initial screening application is required* to assess reasons for entering the teaching profession and dealing with current issues in education. Grade point averages or test scores are not as important as are a candidate's mission, empathy, and experiences with young people.

- Finalists take part in *interviews* with faculty members and *simulations* to assess a candidate's ability to be student-centered and to handle power issues in the classroom.

- Selected candidates (cohort of 20) are *awarded limited scholarship assistance*.

- *Program lasts for about 11 months with 22 weeks of student teaching.* Instead of a final evaluation, the candidates are given up to *50 observations with feedback from university faculty* targeted to give them insight on the spot about their teaching. Theoretical-type courses are presented at the end of the teacher preparation program based on the rationale that experienced adults are more focused on gaining experience in the classroom and using what they already know to help the learning process.

- The program *faculty continues to work with alternate-route teacher for two years*, creating professional development plans cooperatively with the principals of the schools where Project Promise's graduates are placed.

Follow-up studies on this program show that over 90 percent of the Project Promise graduates find teaching jobs each year, and more than 80 percent stay in teaching for at least five years. Faculty involved in this program indicate that the selection process and the intensive performance-based preparation account for the high placement and retention rate of graduates.

In this framework, considerable attention is placed on the Teacher Inductee Career Stage. Similar to the premise that comprehensive classroom management planning and organization is essential in establishing a businesslike and caring climate for students in which to learn, a comprehensive induction plan communicates the school system's professional expectations and creates a supportive network to help all newcomers meet these performance standards in a sustained manner. Research shows that the emphasis on more extensive induction systems has not been a driving force in most school systems. This career juncture provides the groundwork upon which the subsequent career stages are shaped.

Teacher Specialist

The Teacher Specialist career stage, or master teacher phase, begins when teachers have achieved licensure and begin to (a) advance their content knowledge and skill and (b) seek more in-depth understanding of students and their learning needs. They are primarily interested in their own area of specialization and their students. With survival and security attained, teachers now begin to focus on teaching tasks, classroom environment, and job related responsibilities. Steffey et al. (2000), equates this stage to the professional phase in the life cycle of the career teacher. "Professional teachers most frequently seek help and assistance from other teachers. They actively participate in a collegial network for support and guidance. They begin to look beyond the classroom, seeing themselves and their colleagues as part of a broader profession" (p. 8).

Typically, teachers in this stage range in ages from 25 to 35. The young adult is on an exciting search for status, comfort, and happiness in the workplace, family, and friends. Once needs for belonging to a group have been met, motivation shifts from gaining acceptance to becoming a contributing member. Teachers at this career stage may seek out being an admired and visible member of the school community. Status and prestige affirms the individual's competence and value to the group (Glickman, 2000).

How we approach the professional development of the teacher in this stage is a critical factor in the teacher's journey to becoming an expert in her or his field. The goal is to help each teacher become an active change-agent in the teacher's quest to achieve individual growth in his or her practice and to support career advancement that meets the teacher's emerging needs (CPRS Policy

Brief, 1995). Suggestions for future action to promote expert teacher development include the following:

- ◆ Increased intellectual engagement with their subject-matter to deepen insight of key concepts and pedagogical approaches.

- ◆ Balancing both system-wide/school needs and individual teacher interests and needs.

- ◆ Integrating professional development in the work schedule so teachers have the time to share, discuss, and reflect on their practice.

- ◆ Increased and intensive professional development opportunities for teachers serving high-risk students.

- ◆ More focus on long-term investments in teachers' knowledge of subject matter and pedagogy rather than short-term compliance to immediate needs (CPRS Policy Brief, 1995).

Teacher Leader

Teachers entering this career stage are most concerned with the impact of teaching both inside their classroom and outside. The level of concern shifts from just "my students" to "all students." Teacher leadership is not primarily managerial in nature, and its emphasis is mostly on collegiality. Barth (2001) contends that "teachers who become leaders experience personal and professional satisfaction, a reduction in isolation, a sense of instrumentality, and new learnings—all of which spill over into their teaching. As school-based reformers, these teachers become owners and investors in the school, rather than mere tenants " (p. 443).

Arguing that leadership is all about culture formation, Senge (1990) asserts that leadership must be distributed widely throughout an organization: "It is not enough for one or two individuals to develop these skills" (p. 7). We propose that all teachers should be expected to develop into teacher leaders. With 2.2 million teachers needed to supply America's schools, approximately two-thirds of the teaching workforce will be replaced. Barth (2001) asserts that this is a unique opportunity to revamp the profession. What would we want to happen?

Examples of teacher leadership are already evident but not yet widespread. An era of rising expectations has inspired teachers to aspire to more, both for themselves and for their students. Teachers in this career stage step up to the plate and are willing agents of change in their schools and their profession. They must, as Meier (1995) put it, "lead the way toward their own liberation" (p. 599). That will require taking ownership of their own career path and the accompanying challenges and dilemmas.

The typical age range for teachers moving into this career stage is from 30 to 45. Middle adulthood is often characterized by a loss of one's feeling of omnipotence and the realization of one' limitations. It is marked by a time of reexamination of self and a revision of plans, both personal and professional. The middle-aged adult becomes more confident in deciding priorities on what goals he or she can ultimately hope to achieve. By encouraging middle-adulthood teachers to move into teacher leadership roles, the risk of boredom leading to resignation—either from the job or on the job—may diminish. The natural inclination of the middle-aged teacher to reflect and reorder teaching priorities is encouraged and alternatives are given (Glickman, 2000).

The teacher leader stage is also marked by significant contributions to practice. These teachers are able to reflect on the workplace and facilitate growth and change within it for both students and peers. They are the experts in their content area and create safe and supportive learning environments for all students. Barth (2001) further contends that "all teachers can lead. Indeed, if schools are going to become places in which all children are learning, all teachers *must* lead" (p. 444).

Teacher Steward

The Teacher Steward career stage marks the culmination of a professional life filled with accomplishments. This stage, covering ages ranging from 45 to 65, may or may not end with classroom teaching or formal retirement. Teachers at this point in their professional lives may seek opportunities to complete doctoral degrees in their field, serve as curriculum consultants, move into university teacher education programs, or assume formal leadership positions within their school system. They seek to reflect on their expertise, tinker with new ideas, and share insights gained over time. The teacher steward attempts to think about ways to make teaching and learning better for all stakeholders, seeks to protect schools from reforms and approaches that are not in the best interest of school communities, and promotes those changes that are in the best interest of teachers and students.

Teachers in this stage are not burned-out professionals who are "hanging in there" until retirement, nor are they veterans who want to leave the classroom because they couldn't make it into administration or supervision. The acquisition of more than 25 years of experience is valued and given back to the profession in ways that meet the needs of older teachers' desire for consolidating of achievements and identifying one's remaining career objectives.

Linkages to Adult Development and Career Risk Factors

One of the strongest criticisms of the teaching profession is the lack of a staged career path: A career path that affords teachers the ability to advance and be recognized for increased classroom expertise and to capitalize on adult development needs as they mature. This model attempts to address both of these aspects, while also identifying critical risk factors that research shows may impact on teacher retention. Figure 2.4 outlines the proposed career stages, adult development needs, and retention risk factors for each career stage.

In Part II of this book, we present intervention strategies used by colleagues in the field or suggested by the professional literature that indicate a positive effect in reducing or eliminating these risk factors in each career stage.

Figure 2.4. Career Stages, Corresponding Adult Development Needs and Retention Risk Factors

Career Stage	Adult Development Needs	Career Retention Risks
Teacher Inductee Age Range (21 to 25) Traditional	• Modification of relationships with parents and family • Active mastery of the world • Feelings of omnipotence • Search for romance and pursuit of dreams • Natural inclination toward excitement and idealism	• Realization job is more complex than expected • Experiencing failure • Need for acceptance into the teaching community • Need to teach while learning how to teach • Professional isolation • Facing the risk factors for new teachers without a structured induction/mentoring program
Teacher Inductee Nontraditional	• Will vary depending on age group	• Hasty screening and career assessment processes that do not ensure a best fit between candidate's knowledge, skills, and dispositions for teaching • Lack of assistance in job transfer of previous knowledge and skills to teaching situation • Devaluing of previous career experiences and training • Need to be accepted as an equal partner in the learning process • Lack of emphasis on experiential learning and problem solving in the teacher preparation training program

Teacher Specialist Age Range (23 to 35)	• Era of greatest energy, abundance, contradiction and stress • Peak years biologically • A time for status and recognition and occupational advancement • Building an maintaining an initial adult life structure	• Job routine becomes boring; variety in the work nonexistent • No advancements exist • Workload demands and lack of time • Outdated staffing patterns do not accommodate the need for part-time employment for child rearing, professional development leaves, or sabbaticals • Fragmented professional development that does not promote individual teacher input into goal setting, action planning, monitoring, and self-assessment based on personal/professional goals • No incentives or rewards for seeking and attaining expertise
Teacher Leader Age Range (30 to 45)	• Termination of early adulthood and the start of middle adulthood • Advancement to higher status and responsibility is important	• No clear role expansion and expectation for all teachers to move into leadership roles both within and outside the classroom • No strong sense of a learning community • No strong sense that one can make a difference • Workload demands and lack of time • Personal and family role demands • Paralysis by accountability demands • Taboo among peers to accept or show leadership
Teacher Steward Age Range (45 to 65)	• Biological capabilities begin to decline • Senior status in unique worlds and the desire to be responsible not only for own work but also for the development of the current generation of young adults who will soon follow • Key developmental task is the process of individuation. The adult becomes more compassionate, more reflective, more judicious, less ruled by inner conflicts and external demands • Acceptance of life and affiliations • Focus on completing important activities	• Early retirement due to lack of desire to give back to profession • Inability to capitalize on the expertise of the practitioner and redirect where needed in the system • Outdated staffing patterns that do not meet needs of mature teachers who wish to teach part-time and/or assist with developing curriculum and mentoring new teachers

About the Professional Career Framework

The career stages are not necessarily entirely discrete. As teachers mature in age and experience, achieve specific goals, set new objectives, and build self-efficacy within and between career stages, these phases will begin to overlap during transition years. The model presents a career continuum that builds on teacher knowledge and skill, and invites teachers to promote their own internal worth as a teacher and a professional educator. Each career stage, as developed in this guide, suggests the standards and benchmarks teachers can use to channel their journey, challenge their comfort levels, and assess their performance through multiple sources and experiences.

We firmly believe that as adult learners, the only behavior we can change is our own. Our profession has historically suffered from a lack of respect from both internal and external audiences. Perhaps the way to alter this perception is to begin to really toot our own horn and back it with evidence that clearly demonstrates how complex our world really is and how skillful we really are in bringing all students to higher levels of both personal and academic success. Perhaps Meier (1992), in her article "Reinventing Teaching," gives us a path to consider:

> To get where we are now to where we need to be will require teachers to play a substantially different role within their schools as well as in public discourse. Teachers need to relearn what it means to be good in-school practitioners, while also becoming more articulate and self-confident spokespeople for the difficult and often anxiety-producing changes school are expected to undertake. If teachers are not able to join in leading such changes, the changes will not take place. (p. 594)

Uses and Benefits of the Professional Career Framework

For the Profession

This career framework provides teacher education programs, school districts, schools, and teachers with a systematic way to view the long-term professional development of teachers. In this career framework, experienced and new teachers are not treated the same, are not accorded the same status, and are not expected to conform to the same routines. A continuum model of teacher development seeks to replace static views.

For Teacher Preparation Programs

Teacher quality is generally viewed as an important factor in improving student performance in K–12 schools (Murnane & Levy, 1996: Wenglinsky, 1997). Teacher quality at the teacher preparation stage is impacted by the scope and sequence of the teacher education program, teacher certification and licensure processes, and early methods of induction to schools and classrooms. During the pre-service/novice stage of career induction, teacher preparation programs can use this framework to begin the conversation that teaching does have a career path and that all teachers are expected to design and take responsibility for their own professional development throughout their teaching career. Through the development of portfolios linked to standards for beginning teachers (INTASC), teacher preparation programs can begin the newcomer's journey based on a collaborative learning community modeled by the college faculty, cooperating teachers, and peer interactions.

The characteristics of professional learning communities provide the rationale for continuous teacher development based on standards of classroom practice throughout the career path. Darling-Hammond (1997) wrote: "Teaching all children for high levels of understanding will require more intensive teacher training, more meaningful licensure systems, and more thoughtful professional development" (p. 334). Lieberman (2000) tells us "there is a growing body of knowledge from schools that have discovered the power and critical importance of professional development when viewed as an integral part of the life of the school" (p. 2). Concepts and issues related to professional development in schools need to become part of the pre-service and graduate curriculum if sustained teacher development is the goal.

For School Systems and Schools

According to the North Central Regional Educational Laboratory study of state funding for teacher development (Ward et al., 1999), "professional development efforts for teachers can have a more immediate impact than teacher education programs in enhancing the knowledge and skills of the approximately three million public school teachers in the United States today" (p. 3). The professional development of teachers raises several important policy questions concerning responsibility, funding, and program sponsorship. Should the major responsibility for professional development rest with the state, the school district, the individual school, or the teacher? Who should pay and how much should be invested?

In their policy study of state programs for funding teacher professional development, Ward et al. (1999), indicated that states did not seem to play an active role in mandating teacher professional development or supporting with resources. This was explained in the context that such a policy initiative would be very costly. However, in order to have a direct impact on improving teacher quality, many states are developing and implementing new state-funded programs for teacher development (Laitsch, 2001).

For states, school systems, and schools, this framework gives a starting point to begin to gather data about the adult learning, career risk factors, and professional development needs of teachers at each stage of the framework. We think the model can be used as a tool to attract and retain qualified candidates and teachers by appealing to their sense of self-efficacy and actualization within a career in teaching. States and school systems need a planned approach in developing future school principals who come from the teaching ranks. The framework could help states and school systems to begin conversations about putting together all the pieces of the teacher development continuum (i.e., recruitment, selection, preparation, evaluation, career and professional development, and reward).

For Principals and Teachers

Teachers at various career stages may want to focus on gaining subject matter expertise, applying innovative instructional approaches, nurturing other teachers, developing a new curriculum, or pursuing opportunities for both personal and professional growth and achievement. Principals can begin to (a) develop learning communities based on emerging interests and professional inquiry within each career stage; and (b) marshal support and design incentives to help teachers achieve their professional development goals.

The point is this: Teachers who have made significant contributions to their profession across the career continuum tend to be more productive and remain in the profession longer than those who experience job dissatisfaction and quit. We think this model offers a plan to help teachers (a) address their adult and career development needs in a systematic progression and (b) validate their work through customized professional development action plans and supporting artifacts.

References

Adams, R. D., and Martray, C. (1981, April). *Teacher development: A study of factors related to teacher concerns for pre-beginning, and experienced teachers.* Paper presented at the annual meeting of the American Educational Research Association, Los Angeles.

Allen, R. (2001). Kay Awalt Musgrove places primacy on teachers. *ASCD Education Update, 34*(3), 3.

Barth, R. (2001, February). The teacher leader. *Phi Delta Kappan, 82*(6)443–449.

Black, S. (2001, January). Morale matters. *American School Board Journal*. January, 40–43.

Cantor, J (1992). *Delivering instruction to adult learners* (pp. 35–43). Toronto: Wall & Emerson.

Consortium for Policy Research in Education. (1995). *Helping teachers teach well: Transforming professional development.* http://www.ed.gov/pubs/CPRE/t61/t61c.html. Retrieved 11/5/01.

Cranton, P. (1992). *Working with adult learners* (pp. 13–15 and 40–63). Toronto: Wall & Emerson.

Darling-Hammond, L. (1997). *The right to learn: A blueprint for creating schools that work.* San Francisco: Jossey-Bass.

Feiman-Nemser, S., Schwille, S., Carver, C., & Yusko, B. (1999). *A conceptual review of literature on teacher induction.* National Partnerships for Excellence and Accountability in Teaching. Available from: http://www.edpolicy.org.

Gehrke, N. J. (1991). Seeing our way to better helping of beginning teachers. *Educational Forum, 55*(3), 233–242.

Glickman, C., Gordon, S., & Ross-Gordon, J. (2001) *SuperVision and instructional leadership.* Boston, MA: Allyn and Bacon.

Knowles, M. (1994). *The adult learner: A neglected species.* Houston: Gulf Publishing.

Laitsch, D. (2001). Legislative update. *AACTE Education Policy Clearinghouse 1*(1). http://www.edpolicy.org. Retrieved 11/10/01.

Levinson, D. (2001). A conception of adult development. In R. Diessner & J. Tiegs (Eds.), *Human Development* (pp. 296–306). Guilford, CT: McGraw Hill/Dushkin.

Lieberman, A. (2000). *Practices that support teacher development: Transforming conceptions of professional learning.* http://www.her.nsf.gov/HER/REC/pubs/NSF_EF/lieber.htm. Retrieved 11/17/00.

Meier, D. (1992, Summer). Reinventing teaching. *Teachers College Record, 93*(4), 594–609.

Meier, D. (1995). *The power of their ideas.* Boston: Beacon.

Murnane, R. J., & Levy, F. (1996). Evidence from fifteen schools in Austin, Texas. In G. Burtless (Ed.), *Does money matter? The effect of school resources on student achievement and adult success* (pp. 93–96). Washington: Brookings.

Peredo, M. W. (2001). *Directions in professional development: Findings of current literature*. National Clearinghouse for Bilingual Education. http://www.ncbe.gwu.edu

Senge, P. (1990). The leaders new work: Building learning organizations. *Sloan Management Review, 32*(1), 7–22.

Steffey, B. E., Wolfe, M. P., Pasch, S. H., and Enz, B. J. (Eds.). (2000). *Life cycle of the career teacher*. Thousand Oaks, CA: Corwin Press.

Stroot, S., Keil, V., Stedman, P., Lohr, L., Faust, R., Schincariol-Randall, L. et al. (1998). *Peer assistance and review guidebook*. Columbus, OH: Ohio Department of Education.

U.S. Department of Education (1998). *Promising practices: New ways to improve teacher quality*. Available from: http://www.ed.gov/pubs/PromPractice/chapter5.html

Ward, J., St. John, E., & Laine, S. (1999). *State programs for funding teacher professional development*. Oak Brook, IL: North Central Regional Educational Laboratory, 1–17.

Wenglinsky, H. (1997). *When money matters*. Princeton, NJ: Educational Testing Service.

3

Teacher Retention Profile

What Is Your Weakest Link?

Local school districts faced with teacher vacancies are competing with other districts and states for a shrinking pool of teacher candidates. Pre-service teachers interviewing for jobs tell us that many school districts are offering sizeable bonuses, help with real estate costs, and higher starting salaries. In addition, there has been significant growth in providing "nontraditional" potential teachers with opportunities to pursue licensure and teaching careers. The challenge is to maintain quality at a time when quantity is such a strong need.

The National Teacher Recruitment Clearinghouse cautions that though it is important to pay careful attention to attracting individuals to the teaching profession, it is equally important to develop strategies to keep those teachers in the classroom and support their development. They assert that about 30 to 50 percent of teachers leave their jobs within the first five years.

Several questions come to mind: Why do we wait until we have serious teacher shortages before we begin to create innovative and rewarding ways to attract qualified candidates into our profession? Why do we seem to react to problems instead of preventing them? Why do we continue to stand by, year after year, and watch as our new teachers—and even many of our veteran teachers—leave the profession?

The Importance of the School Workplace

In a three-year study of the Montana Beginning Teacher Support Program, the researchers concluded that "beginning teachers take the teaching context they are in very personally" and "the context of the local school is a dominant factor in how the beginner's source of well-being develops" (Spuhler & Zetler, 1995). Yet, knowing this, the professional literature documents that well-planned induction programs are the exception rather than the rule. According to Weiss & Weiss (1999), only eight states in 1984 reported initiating, approving, to 31 in 1991 (Gold, 1996), but as of 1998 stands at 26 states (Andrews & Andrews, 1998). Many states eliminated programs as a result of reduced or restricted funding.

Teacher shortages, in our opinion, will continue unless school communities begin to look at what they do in their schools and begin to shift fundamental beliefs about the work culture. We have learned that schools with high rates of teacher retention have certain characteristics that set them apart from those schools that have more difficulty in keeping new and experienced teachers. The following Teacher Retention Perception Profile inventory, based on these characteristics, is designed to help you analyze the conditions in your school as they relate to the career risk factors that face beginning teachers as well as veteran teachers.

We suggest that all stakeholders might be involved in gathering data and assessing your current situation as it relates to teacher retention. To determine where you want to focus your teacher retention efforts, think critically about your current situation and pinpoint your priorities for improvement. The inventory is intended as a starting place for collaborative dialogue.

Figure 3.1. Teacher Retention Perception Profile Inventory

Schools with high rates of teacher retention have characteristics that set them apart from those schools that have more difficulty in keeping both new teachers and more experienced teachers. This inventory is designed to help you analyze the conditions in your school in relation to ideal patterns as expressed in the current research and professional literature on teacher attrition and retention.

You will read and respond to each statement about the work patterns in your school. Each statement describes the knowledge base, attitude or work activity that relates to five areas linked to teacher retention. After you have responded you may wish to answer the questions at the end of the instrument.

Directions: Respond to each statement. Mark an X in the box that closely corresponds to your perceptions of each statement according to the following scale:

1. Strongly Disagree (SD)
2. Disagree (D)
3. Neutral/No Opinion (N)
4. Agree (A)
5. Strongly Agree (SA)

Area One: Teacher Induction

	1 SD	2 D	3 N	4 A	5 SA
Knowledge Base					
The school/district knows the major components of successful induction programs.					
The school/district knows the potential impact (positive and negative) of teacher induction on teacher retention.					
Dispositions					
The school/district knows and values the importance of a structured and clearly defined teacher induction program.					
The school/district views teacher induction as the first phase in a series of career stages in the professional development of teachers from novices to experts to teacher leaders.					
Work Patterns					

	1	2	3	4	5
The school/district provides a detailed program/orientation of induction that is sustained throughout the year and follows a clear agenda.					
The school/district develops a separate process for the induction of alternate-certification teachers that ensures a best fit between previous career experiences and current demands of teaching in schools.					
The school/district provides support for the induction of new teachers by training mentors and sustaining a teacher mentoring program.					
The school/district finds ways to support teacher mentors through released time, reduced teaching load, and/or financial compensation.					
The school/district has clear vision of effective teaching that is linked to state and national standards.					
The school/district clearly communicates teacher expectations and norms of teacher conduct and performance, orally and in writing.					
The school/district ensures that new teachers receive ongoing supervision, coaching, demonstration, and assessment in preparation for the evaluation component.					
The school/district develops incentives and rewards to promote teacher expertise and development for both new and experienced teachers.					
The school/district links career induction to professional development.					
The school/district implements an Induction Team to develop induction systems and evaluate their impact on teacher attitudes and retention.					
The school/district develops a Beginner Teacher's Handbook to clarify expectations.					
The school/district implements a beginning teacher peer support group that meets regularly.					
Systematic Teacher Induction Total **Count up the X's in each column and then multiply by the number at the top of each column.** Add the totals across and place in the box below.					
Teacher Induction Total					

Area Two: Mentoring New Teachers

	1 SD	2 D	3 N	4 A	5 SA
Knowledge Base					
The principal and staff know the risk factors for new teachers at their school and develop approaches to reduce their impact.					
The principal and staff know the key components in an effective mentoring program.					
The principal/staff/team knows the warning signs that lead new teachers to question their competence and confidence.					
The principal and staff know the key characteristics of new teachers' adult stages of development.					
Dispositions					
The principal and staff accept professional responsibility for mentoring new teachers and all are committed to the process.					
The principal and staff value life long learning for self and others.					
The principal is committed to high quality standards, expectations, and performances.					
Work Patterns					
The principal and the staff together identify the ideal classroom settings and locations for new teachers in order to foster team planning and collaboration (e.g., new teachers are not located in isolated trailers or classrooms).					
The principal and the staff work together to coach and mentor teachers new to the school and the profession.					
The principal and/or the administrative team orients new teachers to the school, presents job expectations and realities, reviews the evaluation system, and provides a mechanism for ongoing communication between the administration and new teachers.					

	1 SD	2 D	3 N	4 A	5 SA
The principal and staff examine the instructional schedule to identify ways to keep it responsive to both new teacher and student needs as it relates to teaching and learning.					
Extracurricular duties and assignments are monitored and kept to a minimum for new teachers.					
The principal/staff/team reviews a new teacher's class schedule and modifies the student composition in each assigned class to make sure it reflects a group that is manageable in the number of "problem" students and academic abilities.					
The principal/staff/team assigns courses and content that matches the current content knowledge and skill level of the new teacher.					
The principal/staff/team monitors the workload (number of preparations, extra duties and assignments) of the new teacher and increases it gradually.					
The principal/staff/team develops a six to nine week notebook or internal Internet bank of past lessons, tests, projects, etc., in the assigned content for the new teacher to use as a planning resource.					
The principal/staff/team monitor the new teacher for negative attitudes and emotions.					
The principal/staff/team provide a communication network to build an open forum for presenting problems about the nature of the job.					
The principal/staff/team implement a problem-solving–problem-setting climate as difficulties emerge.					
The principal/staff/team have a back-up plan to assist the new teacher when current interventions begin to show problems.					
Mentoring New Teachers Total **Count up the X's in each column and then multiply by the number at the top of each column.** Add the totals across the columns and place in box below.					
Mentoring New Teachers Total					

Area Three: Collaboration and Inquiry

	1 SD	2 D	3 N	4 A	5 SA
Knowledge Base					
The principal and staff know the key characteristics of a professional learning community.					
The principal and staff know and understand the practices that support teacher development.					
The principal and staff know research-based principles that should guide professional development					
Dispositions					
The principal and staff value a culture of inquiry and continuous improvement.					
The principal and staff know the importance of teachers' individual and collective responsibility for student learning.					
The principal and staff value data collection and feedback on all aspects of the school's performance.					
Work Patterns					
Teachers talk frequently with one another in a problem-solving, action oriented way about matters of instruction.					
Professional dialogue is viewed as critical in the improvement of schools, increasing student achievement and supporting critical thinking among the staff.					
The principal/staff/team designs ways for teachers to interact with one another on a regular basis. The focus of these interactions is on teaching and learning and how to make it better.					
Common planning periods, regularly scheduled team or subject-area meetings, and released time for collaborative work are built into the master schedule.					

	1 SD	2 D	3 N	4 A	5 SA
Teachers are involved in the decision-making process when it deals with curriculum and instruction.					
New teachers are involved in decision making, and their input is valued.					
The principal/staff/team agrees on professional standards, shares a common purpose, and works together as a community of learners in solving common problems and meeting common goals.					
The principal/staff/team collects data about the school's productivity to help assess strengths and growth areas. This data is shared and the staff assists in planning goals and action plans.					
The principal/staff/team develop both long-term and short-term instructional goals.					
Teachers rely more on current research that informs practice, rather than on personal experiences.					
Teachers are open to a broad range of ideas on collegiality and collaboration with peers, students, and parents.					
Teachers are open to curricular and instructional changes, innovations, and approaches.					
Teachers are encouraged to develop professional networks and collaborations at local, state, and national levels to help them build and refine content knowledge and teaching practices.					
Teachers play a proactive role in designing their own professional plans using appropriate career standards and benchmarks to help them determine goals and assess accomplishments.					
Collaboration and Inquiry Total **Count up the X's in each column and then multiply by the number at the top of each column.** Add the totals across the columns and place in box below.					
Collaboration and Inquiry Total					

Area Four: Teacher Leadership Capacity

	1 SD	2 D	3 N	4 A	5 SA
Knowledge Base					
The principal and staff know and understand the concept of shared leadership.					
The principal and staff know and understand the concept of teacher leadership.					
Dispositions					
The principal and staff believe that all stakeholders need to be involved in leading the school.					
Work Patterns					
Teachers are given time and opportunities to participate in the decision-making processes of the school.					
Teachers value peer collaboration on curriculum and instructional issues.					
Teachers are encouraged to initiate changes that impact on teaching and learning.					
Teachers are encouraged to aspire to leadership, school-wide and beyond.					
Teachers feel that their work contributes to the overall success of the school.					
Teachers are given the time, opportunity, and the expectation to be teacher leaders in their school.					
Leadership is broadly distributed among teachers and administrators.					
New roles for teachers are identified and supported with training, time, and rewards.					
Teacher Leadership Capacity Total **Count up the X's in each column and then multiply by the number at the top of each column.** Add the totals across the columns and place in box below.					
Teacher Leadership Capacity					

Area Five: Professional Development

	1 SD	2 D	3 N	4 A	5 SA
Knowledge Base					
The district/principal and staff know research-based principles/standards that should guide professional development.					
The district/principal and staff know the life cycle of the career teacher.					
Dispositions					
The district/principal and staff view professional development as an on going process over one's career rather than 5 to 7 days of in-service once a year.					
The district/principal/staff/team believes that teaching has distinct developmental career stages, which imply varying professional development approaches. All teachers are not treated the same based on career phase.					
Work Patterns					
The district/principal/staff adopt or develop career stages for teachers to guide professional development.					
The district/principal/staff/team employs processes of reflection and renewal at each stage.					
The district/principal/team designs professional development based on current research findings and behavioral dimensions of adult learning for each stage.					
The district/principal/team assists teachers in becoming active collaborators in their own professional development.					
The district/principal/team assess professional development on the basis of it effects on teacher instruction and student learning, and use this assessment to guide future action planning.					

	1 SD	2 D	3 N	4 A	5 SA
The district/principal/team nurtures the intellectual and leadership capacity of all teachers by enabling teachers to develop further expertise in all essential elements of teaching to higher standards.					
The district/principal/team outlines incentives, rewards, and recognition to support outstanding teaching achievement.					
Professional Development Total **Count up the X's in each column and then multiply by the number at the top of each column.** Add the totals across the columns and place in box below.					
Professional Development Total					

Analysis of Work Patterns

Factor	Highest Score Possible	Current School Score	Calculate Your Percent of the Total	Strength or Growth Target
I Teacher Induction	80			
II Mentoring New Teachers	100			
III Collaboration and Inquiry	100			
IV Teacher Leadership Capacity	55			
V Professional Development	55			
Highest Total Possible	390			

If the highest total is between 320–390

> Virtually all your knowledge, attitudes, values, and work patterns are characteristic of schools with higher levels of teacher retention at all career levels.

If the highest total is between 240–320

> The majority of your knowledge, attitudes, values, and work patterns are characteristic of schools with high levels of teacher retention at all career levels. You may have areas that can be fine-tuned.

If the highest total is between 160–240

> Some of your knowledge, attitudes, values, and work patterns are characteristic of schools with high levels of teacher retention at all career levels. Many are not. You may need to reassess.

If the total is less than 160

> Few of your knowledge, attitudes, values, and work patterns are characteristic of schools with high levels of teacher retention.

Graph Your Results

Factors	0 to 20 percent	20 to 40 percent	40 to 60 percent	60 to 80 percent	80 to 100 percent
Teacher Induction					
Mentoring New Teachers					
Collaboration and Inquiry					
Teacher Leadership Capacity					
Professional Development					

Career Maps: Pathways For School Improvement

Throughout this guide, we provide career maps to assist you in thinking about what you do and comparing it to current trends and practices as it relates to teacher retention and career development. We do not attempt to tell you what to do or how to accomplish a particular task. We believe that planning, revising, and implementing any new program resides with those who must make it happen.

Our goal is to tackle your way of thinking and provide resources and guidelines for collaborative work sessions with staff. As adult learners, we know we learn best when we perceive a need that relates to accomplishing goals that we think are important. As the school leader and staff developer, you are invited to use these career maps to guide your journey.

Career Map 3.1. Teacher Retention Profile Analysis

What Patterns Do You Observe?

This career map invites you to reflect on what you have learned after completing the Teacher Retention Profile. The goal is to help you identify the strengths your school demonstrates as well as the challenges you face. The Profile Analysis Worksheets that follow in Figure 3.2 present guiding questions and ask you to begin the task of developing a concise critique of your school's ability to attract and retain teachers. The next step, should you decide to continue, is to begin devising or revising a plan for comprehensive school improvement in the areas assessed in the profile. These areas are discussed more fully in later chapters.

To check your perceptions, you might consider giving the Teacher Retention Profile to your staff and compare your responses. Use the data to begin future planning for developing or enhancing your work culture as it relates to teacher induction and retention.

Figure 3.2. Profile Analysis Worksheets

Guiding Questions—Strongest Links

- Which areas do you perceive are your greatest strengths in keeping new teachers?

- Which areas do you perceive are your greatest strengths in keeping experienced teachers?

- What evidence do you have to support your findings?

Guiding Questions—Weakest Links

- Which areas do you perceive to be the weakest link(s) in keeping teachers and therefore require considerable attention?

- How would you prioritize them? What is most important to you?

- What evidence do you have to support your findings?

Guiding Questions—School Retention Profile

- What is your teacher retention profile in your school system and in your school? How many beginning teachers, or teachers new to your school/system, do you lose within the first three years? Why?

- How many experienced teachers leave and why?

- What recommendations for improving teacher induction and retention in your school do you have?

- What barriers do you expect in moving forward on improving teacher retention in your school?

References

Andrews, T. E., & Andrews, L. (Eds/) 1998. TNASDTEC Manual 1998–1999. *Manual on the Preparation and Certification of Educational Personnel*. Dubuque, IA: Kendall-Hunt.

Feiman-Nemser, S., Schwille, S., Carver, C., & Yusko, B. (1999). *A conceptual review of literature on teacher induction*. National Partnerships for Excellence and Accountability in Teaching. Available from: http://www.edpolicy.org.

Furtwengler, C. B. (1995*).* Beginning teachers programs: Analysis of state actions during the reform era. *Education Policy Archives, 3*(3). Available from: http://epaa.asu.edu/epaa/v3n3.html

Gold, Y. (1996). Beginning teacher support: Attrition, mentoring, and induction. In C. B. Courtney (Ed.), *Review of Research in Education, 16,* (pp. 548–594). Washington, DC: American Educational Research Association.

Hord, S. (1997). Professional learning communities: What they are and why they are important. *Issues About Change,* Austin, TX: Southwest Educational Development Lab. 6(1).

Lieberman, A. (2000). Practices that support teacher development: Transforming conceptions of professional learning. http://www.her.nsf.gov/HER/REC/pubs/NSF_EF/lieber.htm. Retrieved 11/17/00.

Little, J. W. (1996). Excellence in professional development and professional community. National Specialty in School Change: Key Issues: Selected Readings About Student Learning. http://www.org/scpd/natspecl/excellecne.html

Peredo, M. W (2001). Directions in professional development: Findings of current literature. National Clearinghouse for Bilingual Education. http://www.ncbe.gwu.edu. Retrieved.

Spuhler, L., & Zetler, A. (1995). Montana beginning teacher support program: Research report for year three 1994–95. ERIC Document ED 390803.

Weiss, E. M., & Weiss, S. C. (1999). Beginning teacher induction. ERIC Document ED 436487.

II

Professional Career Framework

CAREER STAGE

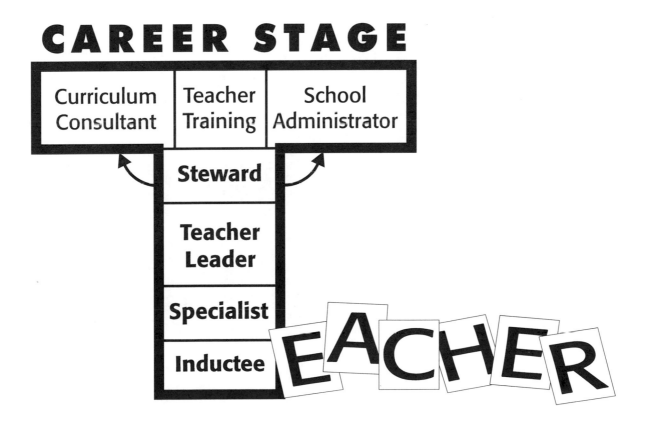

Career
Stage One:
Teacher Inductee

4

Career Induction

How we treat the least experienced among us is a reflection of how we feel about ourselves as a profession. The importance given to teacher induction is a barometer of our professional self-esteem.

Newton et al., 1998,
Mentoring: A Resource and
Training Guide

Think about the quotation above. What does it mean to you?

Teacher Induction

It's always hard to be the new kid on the block, and, no matter how old we are or how experienced we may be, establishing ourselves within new groups is both stressful and challenging. The new teacher comes into the profession ready to learn, willing to collaborate, enthusiastic about teaching as a career, and committed to making a difference in the lives of children. How are we going to capitalize on the attributes new teachers bring while assisting them to develop their teaching knowledge and skills? The changeover from pre-service experiences to first-year teaching "is perhaps the most complex intellectual and emotional transition on the continuum of teacher development" (Steffey et al., 2001, p. 4).

The first career stage (described earlier in Chapter 2), *Teacher Inductee*, is the foundation for the other career stages that will follow in the framework we propose. What the inductee learns about teaching and learning, taking ownership in his or her professional development, and building collaborative relationships during the first three years will have dramatic results: first, in making the critical decision to remain in the profession, and, second, in becoming a self-actualized and competent educator.

Let's Talk Induction

The literature on teacher retention tells us that more than 20 percent of public school teachers leave their positions within three years and almost 10 percent quit before finishing their first year. The increasing shortages of teachers in our schools across the nation is climbing steadily, forcing schools to look internally at what they can do to keep both new and experienced teachers in the profession. Perhaps for the first time, schools are beginning to realize that past indifference toward the way new teachers are socialized into the profession has come back to haunt us.

Systematic and comprehensive induction programs are the exception rather than the trend, and informal induction experiences have been linked with higher levels of teacher attrition as well as lower levels of teacher effectiveness (National Commission on Teaching America's Future, 1996). There is, conversely, more evidence that school systems are beginning to study their induction practices for new teachers (Fideler & Haselkorn, 1999). A national survey in 1998 (Forgionne, 1999) indicated that 34 percent of the teaching faculty in public schools had participated in some form of induction during their first year. Darling-Hammond reported that in 1997, 55 percent of new teachers with less than five years of experience indicated they participated in a formalized induction program in their school setting.

Andrea's Journal

No one graduates from college and begins a chosen career thinking they will be washed out and unsatisfied after five years. Dreams would have to unfulfilled and disappointment very high. Just looking at my school, I can see that too many beginning teachers are experiencing these exact problems. Formal induction programs have been proven to reduce the exiting of teachers new to the teaching profession.... When I look back on my own personal lack of guidance coupled with complete fear of the unknown, I am more willing to develop skills to help others. I wonder why we haven't done a better job....

Miriam's Journal

The professional literature shows that states in which teacher induction programs are formalized have higher retention rates than states that do not. I believe that this evidence should be enough to help school systems make needed changes in their induction policies. Teacher leaders need to voice strongly that induction practices must be valued by the entire school community. Teacher retention is a problem na-

tionwide. As a teacher leader, I hope to do my part in making the necessary changes that will help new teachers be more successful during their early years....

What is Induction and Who Are Inductees?

How you define teacher induction may decide how your overall induction program is designed. Narrow interpretations tend to focus more on survival purposes and easing the transition into the job realities of teaching, whereas broader, more comprehensive interpretations tend to focus more on building teacher quality, professional self-actualization, and collaborative interactions.

What does induction mean to you?
What does your induction program look like? List all the activities teachers new to the system and to your school participate in.
What types of outcomes do you anticipate as a result of these activities?
What would you say best describes the purposes of your induction program?

Limited interpretations of teacher induction often result in one-shot orientation programs before preplanning that present system-level policies, procedures, and expectations. The primary purpose is orientation to the school system; information giving is the general approach, and information overload is usually the result. More comprehensive approaches are more developmental with a specific schedule of system-level orientation topics/activities sequenced over the school year and reinforced at the school level by the administrative team and teacher mentors.

These approaches also focus more on the developmental needs of beginning teachers and reflect more of the key components for systematic and effective induction programs. Purposes of induction in these programs include not only orientation to the setting, but also goals to improve professional practice, develop a learning community, and orient new teachers to long-term career goals.

Inductees are defined as individuals who are new to a job, a situation, or a profession. Traditionally, we have looked at teacher inductees as those who are new to the profession—first-year teachers—but recent definitions have expanded to included (a) pre-service teachers who are first placed into field labs and practicums; (b) alternate-route certification teachers; and (c) those experienced teachers who may be new to a subject, grade level, certification level, or school district.

We think the time is right for teacher educators and school communities to think long and hard at the way we have conducted business in the area of teacher induction. It's time to think about teacher induction from pre-service through in-service. This means viewing pre-service education as the beginning of a continuum that spans the entire career of a teacher—indeed, as the first step in an evolving process. It also means viewing in-service as a way to expect teachers to become active designers in the development of mutual professional development goals and providing the support to help them achieve those objectives.

> **What are your thoughts about induction as a continuum of professional development? Is there a relationship between these two components?**

Why Do We Need Structured and Comprehensive Induction Programs?

A review of the literature shows that schools have established teacher induction programs over the past twenty years to both orient and retain new teachers. Numerous studies document the value of teacher induction programs and describe a variety of program designs for implementation. However, "within the states that have created programs for beginning teachers, local school districts are not always required to offer the programs, nor are all teachers required to participate" (Weiss & Weiss, 1999, p. 1). Likewise there is no consensus in the profession about what new teachers should know and be able to do and what constitutes the best way to accomplish this task.

The research is consistent in reporting that those school systems that have developed sustained induction programs are reaping positive results (Serpell & Bozeman, 1999). A well-planned program can make the difference in teacher retention, the development of the type of the teacher you want to have in your classrooms, and, ultimately, the type of learning experience you target for all students. The bottom line is this: A strong support system for a beginning teacher, an experienced teacher new to your school, or an experienced teacher making the transition into another career stage, can mean the difference between the teacher staying or leaving, and will have your school fostering the type of career development that results in highly productive and self-actualized professionals (National Teacher Recruitment Clearinghouse, 2000).

In the following career maps, we have targeted four objectives to help guide your analysis of your current induction program. By the end of this chapter, you should be able to:

1. Assess/develop your definition of teacher induction
2. Clearly articulate teacher induction motives and purposes
3. Analyze current induction program for key components and effectiveness
4. Investigate a comprehensive induction program to meet school improvement goals

In Figure 4.1 you will find a checklist that identifies eight key components used in effective induction programs and supported by current reform initiatives. Think about your induction system and check the components you currently have. Indicate what evidence you have to verify its presence and effectiveness. Check those components you do not have. Indicate why these aspects should be included in your current induction program.

Research Highlights on Effective Teacher Induction Programs

There is growing data to support notions of what makes a good induction program. Schlechty (1985) presents a checklist of eight program guidelines to help schools develop and assess their induction programs:

1. Explain to the inductees that the process of their selection is based on special requirements and that induction training is critical to their success.
2. Divide the induction process into progressive stages of achievement
3. Cultivate mutual support with the peer groups
4. Orient toward long-term career goals
5. Clearly articulate and disseminate administrative expectations and teacher conduct
6. Teach and help inductees assimilate the professional vocabulary
7. Provide supervision, coaching, demonstration, and assessment
8. Involve total faculty in the supervision of the inductee in a tightly organized, consistent, and continuous program.

Camp & Health-Camp (1991) examined the induction process for vocational education teachers in a research study and proposed ten major components for an induction assistance program:

1. Professional development center
2. Local professional development coordinator
3. Detailed orientation
4. Structured mentoring program
5. Beginning teachers handbook
6. Beginning teacher support group
7. Systematic administrator support
8. Flexible series of ongoing in-service workshops
9. Certification coursework for alternative certification teachers
10. Coaching in reflective teaching

Career Map 4.1.

Figure 4.1. Existing Induction Program Checklist

Components	Yes	No	Why Needed
Clear Program Description			
Definition of Teacher Induction			
• Narrow in scope			
• Broad in scope			
Purposes of Teacher Induction clearly stated and communicated			
Designated Coordinator			
Induction Coordinator • Responsibility of induction/mentoring planning and implementation specifically assigned to a staff member or induction team.			
Detailed Orientation Program			
• To the School System			
• To the Assigned School			
• To the Assigned Team/Grade/Subject			
• Implemented over the School Year			
Beginning Teacher Handbook			
Structured Mentoring Program			
• Clear selection criteria for mentors			
• Structured training program for mentors			
• Planned staff development activities to support mentoring program			
• Program evaluation relating to goals and objectives			
Systematic Administrative Support			
System Level			
• Provide necessary financial and human resources to support induction goals and activities			
• Clearly articulate and disseminate administrative expectations and teacher conduct			

• Compensate trained mentors and provide opportunities for professional growth			
School Level			
• Initiate a teacher induction team to plan, monitor, and assess induction processes at the school			
• Involve total faculty in the supervision of the inductee.			
• Provide ongoing and systematic communication between administration and inductees.			
• Provide mentors the time to perform key mentoring tasks through release time			
Collaboration With Local Universities			
• Seek and assist with pre-service field placements			
• Collaborate to retain and develop teachers over the career path			
Oriented Toward Long-Term Career Goals			
• The induction program is part of a larger effort to keep, develop, and promote teachers within the profession			
• The use of individual professional development plans and action planning is utilized to foster a proactive approach to career and adult development			
• Incentives and rewards throughout the career path are clearly targeted.			

Now that you have had a chance to review these characteristics of effective induction programs, are there any aspects of teacher induction you think should be added to your program?

What benefits do you foresee by revising your current induction system?

What questions come to mind?

According to the Educational Commission of the States (2001), a number of studies have shown that induction programs are valuable in enhancing teaching effectiveness and increasing the retention rate of new teachers. Review of these programs show they exhibit the following six characteristics:

1. Use experienced and well-trained teachers as mentors
2. Are guided by well defined program standards
3. Are adequately funded
4. Include an assessment process for new teachers
5. Extend beyond the first year of a teacher's career
6. Are part of a larger effort to keep, develop, and promote teachers within the profession

Similarly, *Promising Practices: The Induction of New Teachers* (2000), gives five characteristics for promising induction programs:

1. Give special attention to new teachers in an effort to link their performance to high standards
2. Collaborate with universities and schools to create learning contexts for beginning teachers. The relationship is viewed as mutually beneficial for both teacher and college faculty in the area of professional development.
3. Often take place in an extended fifth year of graduate study in which practice teaching is combined with seminars and coursework
4. Satisfy licensure and certification requirements, but also provide assistance with everyday problems and encourage new teachers to be reflective about their work.
5. Compensate trained mentors and provide opportunities for professional growth, such as becoming adjunct faculty at college campuses.

Career Map 4.2.
Designing Your Teacher Induction Program

We suggest that the first step you take is to increase teacher retention is to initiate a New Teacher Induction Team/Committee at the system/school level. Teacher induction/mentoring has been identified as an effective (quick fix) way to assist beginning teachers, but the strategy is not clearly linked to strategic organizational and school improvement goals. This step, in our opinion, has been overlooked in the process of trying to halt new-teacher flight. This team might be composed of teacher educators from the local university/college, administrators, teacher mentors, and first-year teachers who have a special interest in the professional development of all teachers.

The purpose of the team would be to: (a) study the multiple meanings of induction and key components, (b) design an induction program in your school that is comprehensive, developmental, sustained, and evaluated, (c) identify the risk factors for new teachers in your school and devise ways to eliminate or minimize, and (d) develop a career mapping plan aimed at keeping all stakeholders actively involved in professional development over the span of the teaching career. We feel the use of an induction team can better assist the school in involving all faculty in the induction process. This strategy would also help assigned mentor teachers by allowing them to focus more on teaching and classroom management issues.

Organizing the Induction Team

Review Figure 4.2 for a list of stakeholders and the type of support that is needed in order to develop and sustain an induction program. Revise the table to include additional stakeholders and the types of support they can provide.

Several activities are presented here that the team can utilize to build its knowledge base about teacher induction in order to make informed decisions.

Figure 4.2. Creating the Induction Team

Stakeholder	Support Needed
School Board Members Superintendent	• Provide political base and moral support for the program • Assist in delegating resources to support program goals • Recognize publicly those who develop and implement the program
Central Office Staff Development Director Principal	• Develop the criteria for selecting mentors • Design the mentor teacher training program • Recruit mentors • Provide support for mentors • Find ways to reward and recognize mentors • Evaluate the impact of the mentoring program on the entire school community • Assess beginners and work with mentors to help new teachers build on teaching strengths and improve growth areas through careful action planning
Teacher Mentors	• Willing to provide direct assistance to peers • Collaborate with other mentors to share ideas and problems • Seek data on the impact of their mentoring on mentee and on student achievement of mentee's classes • Become skilled in cognitive coaching and the tasks of mentoring
Other Teachers	• Form a support network for mentors by opening their classrooms for visits by beginners and co-teaching with them • Assist in socializing the new teacher to the school's procedures and norms • Help in reducing risk factors for new teachers and in establishing conditions that give beginners the best chance for success.
University Faculty	• Assist the induction team in program development • Help train mentors • Provide staff development • Update mentors and school staff on current research in teacher education that impacts first-year teachers.

Figure 4.3. Teacher Induction—Information Search

Activity One

Conduct a review of the literature on teacher induction. Here are several sources that might prove helpful in assisting the team in learning the current trends and problems associated with Beginning Teacher Induction.

Ed Policy Research Resource
http://www.edpolicy.org
Click-Induction/Mentoring

- Beginning Teacher Induction: A Report on Beginning Teacher Effectiveness and Retention (Serpell & Bozeman, 1999)
- The Effects of Exemplary Teacher Induction Programs (Feiman-Nemser et al., 1999)

Education Policy Analysis Archives
http://epaa.usu.edu

- Beginning Teacher Programs (Furtwengler, 1995)

Activity Two

Obtain copies of the following book to learn more about a comprehensive approach to teacher induction and professional development based on career stages.

- *Life Cycle of the Career Teacher.* (Steffy, Wolfe, Pasch, Enz (Eds.), 2000). Corwin Press; e-mail orders: order@corwinpress.com

Activity Three

Plan a group discussion to reach consensus about teacher induction. Use these questions as a way to guide your conversation:

- How does the team define teacher induction? What are the purposes for the program?
- What components of an effective teacher induction program does the team feel are essential? Duplicate the Existing Induction Program Checklist (see Figure 4.1) and use as a guide for discussion.
- What type of induction program should be developed to meet both immediate needs of beginning teachers and long-term professional development needs?
- Compare group reactions to the text outlining specific stages of teacher development (Inductee, Specialist, Teacher Leader, Steward). How does this information influence your thoughts about teacher induction?

Figure 4.4. Teacher Induction—Problem Formulation

Activity Four

Based on your survey results, information search, and group discussion, identify what you feel are key problem areas in the area of teacher induction for your school and school system.

Problems	Factual Support	Opinions and Feelings	Desired Results	Best Solution(s)
Problem #1				
Problem #2				
Problem #3				

Support your problem identification with both facts and opinions about your school. Prioritize these problem areas.

Brainstorm a list of desired results.

Select best solution(s) based on need and resources available.

Figure 4.5. Teacher Induction—Action Plan

Activity Five

Once you have clearly defined the key problem areas, develop an action plan to guide the implementation of your emerging teacher induction program.

Problem	Target Solution	Activities to Implement Solution	Person Responsible	Timeline	Evaluation/ Impact on Teacher Retention

Notes:

Career Map 4.3.
Multi-Level Orientation Program Planning

Most school systems conduct orientation activities for beginning teachers and experienced teachers new to the school district. General procedures and documentation, such as required records and paperwork, parental communication policies, ways of securing materials, and reporting student misbehavior, are common administrative concerns for beginning teachers. In addition to system-level policies and procedures, relationships with other staff members and school administrators often concern the new teacher. These new teachers have a strong need to be accepted and viewed as contributing members of the school community.

Orientation activities, therefore, also need to focus on establishing and building professional connections based on cooperation and team building (Webb, Montello, Norton, 1994). **The culture of professional isolation must be attacked on all fronts if we are to keep and retain the teachers selected into the profession.** Discussions with teachers confirm that these activities do provide new personnel with necessary information but often do not specify the personal assistance and support also available to staff members.

This career map invites you to study your orientation program and decide if it includes both aspects of information and team-building components. Consider using large, general sessions for information dissemination, and smaller, break-out sessions for team building and fostering communication links with key central office staff and local administrators. *Consider what information the new teacher needs right now and what can be communicated at a later date.*

Figure 4.6. New Teacher Orientation Agenda and Activities

Take into account the purposes identified in the research that are included in more comprehensive approaches to Teacher Induction:

♦ Orientation to the Setting

♦ Improvement of Professional Practices

♦ Development of the School as a Learning Community

♦ Orientation to Long-Term Career Goals

Target topics and activities you think should occur at each level. Make sure you balance what the system needs to communicate and what beginning teachers and experienced teachers new to your school/system may need. Begin to view the induction process as an interrelated system between the district and the school that supports new teachers over a sustained period of time.

Topic/Date	System Level	School Level	Team/Grade
August			
September			
October			
November			
December			
January			
February			
March			
April			
May			
June			

Now let's look at a new teacher orientation program proposed and implemented by some of our colleagues. As you read this example *highlight the aspects you like* and would consider including in your induction program. *Compare your current program* to this one. *What similarities and differences do you observe?*

Career Map 4.4.
Analysis of New Teacher Orientation Program—Sample Program

Figure 4.7. New Teacher Orientation Program

The Burke County Public Schools feel, that in our quest to equip and retain the best teachers possible, we must provide support and resources even before the first day of school. For this reason, we believe that a New Teacher Orientation Program is essential.

Participants

All first-year Initial Licensure Teachers (ILT) in the Burke County Schools will be required to attend the five-day New Teacher Orientation Program. All teachers with any previous experience that are new to Burke County may attend on a voluntary basis.

The mentors for ILTs will be invited to participate for two and one-half days of the program. All mentors will be involved in a one-half day seminar on the duties and the responsibilities of a mentor, which we believe will help the school system respond to the many questions that mentors have about what is expected of them. The seminar is also a way to provide mentors with strategies on how to help a beginning teacher.

For two days, the mentors will be involved with their mentees at the school site where an orientation will take place and the mentors will help alleviate many of the ILTs' fears. During these two days, the mentors will also be responsible for helping mentees develop lesson plans for the first week of school, organize the classroom, and assist in obtaining necessary supplies.

Activities

The five-day New Teacher Orientation Program will be superior to the normal orientation provided to most new teachers: "Here are your keys, there is your room, and good luck." The orientation program should provide new teachers with strategies and techniques that will give them a distinct advantage over other beginning teachers. This program will provide preparation time for teachers, reduce their anxiety level, and will allow them to be ready for students when they enter the class. There will be an *Issue Bin* for participants to provide suggestions and ask questions during each day of the program. This will provide participants the opportunity to share concerns anonymously. The program will be structured as follows:

Day One: July—8 A.M. to 4 P.M.

Goal: To acquaint all teachers new to the Burke County Schools with the school system's philosophy, procedures, and culture.

Program:

- Registration/Reception (Members of the school board and other school system employees will be invited.)

- Welcome and Introduction of Guests—Associate Superintendent

- Philosophy and Goals of the Burke County Schools—Superintendent

- Discussion With Program Directors

  - *Director of Program Services and Elementary Education*

  - *Director of Program Services*

  - *Director of Secondary Education*

  - *Director of Exceptional Education*

  - *Coordinator of AG/Middle School Curriculum*

  - *Director of Child Nutrition*

  - Director of Vocational Education

  - Director of Transportation

  - *Director of Maintenance*

- Finance and Payroll—Assistant Superintendent

- What Does It Mean To Be an Employee of the Burke County Schools?

- Teacher of the Year—Video

- Teacher to Teacher—Panel Discussion

- Panel Members—Teacher of the Year Recipients and Nominees

- Management and Organization—The Effective Teacher (In-Service Video with Harry Wong—Parts 1 and 2)

Lunch will be provided—attendees will be grouped according to grade level for lunch.

Day Two: July—8 A.M. to 4 P.M.

Goal: To supply all teachers new to the Burke County Schools with necessary instructional strategies, organizational strategies, and classroom management techniques that will enhance the probability of their success. To provide mentors an orientation on their role and responsibilities.

Program: Concurrent Sessions

- School Law for Teachers
- Teaching Strategies for the Elementary Teacher
- Reading Strategies for Middle/Secondary Teachers
- Exceptional Children Issues
- Teaming in the Middle School
- Teaching Strategies for the 90-Minute Block—High School Teachers
- Strategies for Successful Mentoring
- Discipline Strategies for Teachers (In-Service Video with Harry Wong—Parts 3 and 4)

Breakout sessions will be held for elementary, middle, and high school teachers. Experienced mentors will be conducting the breakout sessions.

Lunch will be provided—attendees will be grouped according to grade level.

Day Three: July—8 A.M. to 4 P.M.

Goal: To familiarize all new teachers with the Burke County Schools, create an awareness of available resources, and orientate them to their home school.

Program:

- Develop Effective Lessons—The Effective Teacher (Parts 5 and 6)
- Tour the Burke County Schools on Buses

All new teachers meet their mentors at their home school for an orientation and to begin preparing for the first week of school.

All new teachers will meet individually with their principals.

Needed supplies will be requested and available supplies will be provided.

Day Four: July—8 A.M. to 4 P.M.

Goal: To allow all teachers new to the Burke County Schools time with their mentors at their home school to prepare for the first day and first week of school.

Program:

- ◆ Mentors will assist new teachers in preparing for the first day of school

- ◆ ILTs and mentors will prepare pacing guides

- ◆ ILTs will prepare lesson plans for the first week of school with their mentors

- ◆ The course of study for the grade level will be reviewed and discussed

- ◆ Strategies for assessing and evaluating students will be addressed

Day Five: July—8 A.M. to 4 P.M.

Goal: To prepare ILTs for the many responsibilities that come with teaching, to provide information that will enhance the professionalism of teachers, and to review and evaluate what was learned.

Program:

- ◆ Review Instructional Checklist and Characteristics of Outstanding Teachers

The Teacher as Professional—The Effective Teacher Video (Parts 7 & 8)

- ◆ Participants will role play: Parent/Teacher Conferences; What Have We Learned this Week?—Group Skit Lessons from the Book, the *First Day of School*

- ◆ The Assessment and Evaluation of Teachers (Review of INTASC Standards and Implications)

- ◆ Wrap-Up and Evaluations

Lunch by grade levels.

Continue Support Of Participants

- ◆ In order to provide the much needed support for new teachers, the Burke County Schools will provide monthly follow-up sessions that will allow for needed assistance and an opportunity to reflect on recent experiences. Seminars, programs offered, and guest speakers will be based on suggestions from the ILTs (e.g., parent conferences in October, learning styles, using technology, assessment strategies, how to "figure" grades, the ABC Incentive Program, and discipline strategies).

- ILTs will be given opportunities to observe experienced teachers and to establish a communication network with other new teachers, providing an opportunity to share their "best ideas."

- ILTs will be given renewal credit for attending these follow-up sessions. The follow-up sessions will provide all ILTs a foundation for professional growth and development.

Many induction programs design special handbooks for beginning teachers to help them become familiar with the induction process and to outline the support provided in the first two to three years. Figure 4.8 provides a sample *Table of Contents* from such a handbook developed in North Carolina. Review the contents and jot down what you like about this approach. What does this handbook reflect about what the schools in North Carolina value about teacher induction and how beginning teachers' content knowledge and skills are developed?

Career Map 4.5.
Beginning Teacher Handbook

Figure 4.8. Beginning Teacher Handbook Table of Contents

North Carolina Beginning Teacher Handbook August 2001 Table Of Contents	*Your Comments and Reflections*
Introduction • To the Beginning Teacher • How to Use This Handbook • What is Performance-Based Licensure? • Commonly Used Terms • Initial Licensure Program Timetable • What to Do in Year One • Developing a Relationship with Your Mentor • Beginning Teacher Individual Growth Plan **INTASC Standards** • An Introduction to the INTASC StandardsThe INTASC Standards • The INTASC Standards and Key Indicators • Samples of Evidence and Artifacts **Reflection Cycle** • The Reflective Practitioner • The Reflection Cycle • Becoming Reflective Practitioner • Practice Reflection-Cycle Questions about a Lesson **Video Tips** • Videotaping for Reflection and Self-Assessment • Video Self-Assessment Activity **PBL Tool Kit** • Parent/Guardian Contact Log • Log of Discipline Incidents • Professional Development and Contribution Log • Beginning Teacher Individual Growth Plan **Appendix** • Code of Professional Practice and Conduct for North Carolina Educators	

Visit the following Web site to review the complete North Carolina Beginning Teacher Handbook and each of the topics listed above:

http://www.ncpublicschools.org/pbl/pbl_manual.pdf

> **What value would this component bring to your school or school system? Draft a *Table of Contents* for your Beginning Teacher Handbook. What do you think it should include? What reasons guided your choosing of these topics?**

Summary

To conclude this chapter on teacher induction, here are the voices of teacher leaders who have investigated current conditions in their schools. This is what they have to say on the issue:

Michelle's Journal

Education has been described as a profession that eats its young. The isolation of new teachers with no support has been the norm for years. Statistics show that one-third of all new teachers nationwide leave the profession within the first five years. Even with official mentoring programs within a system, veteran teachers need to do more and pick up the slack.

Elaine's Journal

Trends come and go in education. I hope that the steps being taken to nurture beginning teachers through the first years of the teaching profession become policy and not a passing trend. I have always tried to assist new teachers but I now realize that I have not done enough. In fact, we as a profession have not done enough….Perhaps as we, as teacher leaders, become more aware of what is going on in other systems to induct new teachers, we can be instrumental in bringing such essential improvements to our own systems….

Wanda's Journal

I have been a teacher for 20 years and try to learn new things each year. I have always been one to help others, whether it was in a formal or informal setting. Becoming part of this cohort in teacher leadership has given me a new perspective and a new zeal for my profession. Now, I have the research to back the ideas that I felt were important for years. It is so important to help new teachers. We must look at what we do in our schools to make induction a worthwhile and effective process for our new colleagues....

Joyce's Journal

I know first-hand that induction and mentoring are critical to the success of teachers. It is something that I think should be an ongoing aspect of any educational institution. It is important that teachers share and relate to each other on both formal and informal levels. We need to become mentors for each other on a continual basis. Who else out there is cheering for us?

References

Camp, W. G., & Health-Camp, B. (1991). *On becoming a teacher: They just gave me a key and said, "Good luck."* ERIC Document ED335517.

Darling-Hammond, L. (1997). *Doing what matters most: Investing in quality teaching.* New York: National Commission on Teaching & America's Future.

Education Commission of the States. (October-November 2000). New imperatives for teacher preparation, *Teacher preparation and induction, 2(3).* Denver, CO: Education Commission of the States. http://ecs.org/clearinghouse/22/38/ 2238.htm. Retrieved 5/20/01.

Feiman-Nemser, S., Schwille, S., Carver, C., & Yusko, B. (1999). *A conceptual review of literature on new teacher induction.* National Partnership for Excellence and Accountability in Teaching. Available from: http://www.edpolicy.org

Fideler, E., & Haselkorn, D. (1999). *Learning the roles: Urban teacher induction practices in the United States.* Belmont, MA: Recruiting New Teachers.

Forgione, P. D. (1999, April). *Teacher quality in U.S. data on preparation and qualifications.* Press release.

National Commission on Teaching & America's Future. (1996). *What matters most: Teaching for America's Future.* New York: Author, Teachers College, Columbia University.

National Teacher Recruitment Clearinghouse. (2000). *Induction programs.* Available from: http://www.recrutingteachers.org/findteachers/induction.html

Serpell, Z., & Bozeman, L. (1999). *Beginning teacher induction: A report on beginning teacher effectiveness and retention.* National Partnership for Excellence and Accountability in Teaching. Available from: http://www.edpolic.org

Schlechty, P. (1985, January–February). A Framework for evaluating introduction into teaching, *Journal of Teacher Education, 36*(1), 37–41.

Steffey, B. E., Wolfe, M. P., Pasch, S. H., and Enz, B. J. (Eds.). (2000). *Life cycle of the career teacher.* Thousand Oaks, CA: Corwin Press.

U.S. Department of Education. (1998). *Promising practices*: *The induction of new teachers* Available from: http://www.ed.gov/pubs/PromPractice/chapter5.html

Webb, L. D., Montello, P. A., & Norton, M. S. (1994). *Human resources administration.* New York: Macmillan College Publishing.

Weiss, E. M., & Weiss, S. G. (1999). *Beginning teacher induction.* ERIC Clearinghouse on Teaching and Teacher Education Washington, DC: ERIC Document ED436487.

5

Reducing the Risk Factors

Profile of the Teacher Inductee— Knowing Enough for Now

Tina's Journal

As a first-year teacher, I must have heard a thousand times in the past nine months, "Wait until winter break…," and "If you can just make it until spring break…," and "You'll be amazed at what an expert teacher you'll feel like when you return from summer break." And finally I've reached the summer break and I have the chance to not do anything even remotely related to school; and, yet, I'm feeling this desire to reflect on my first year of teaching and where I'm at in my career. I ask my students to do this all the time, shouldn't I do the same?

Well it's safe to say that I've got the patterns and habits down that work for me:

- Put the desk in rows for attendance and daily activities; move to groups or circle when necessary.

- Don't check my voice mail until the end of the day; a disgruntled parent will only "vampirize" all of my energy first thing in the morning.

- Dress like a professional.

- Laugh a lot.

- Take time for myself each day-school will absolutely engulf me if I don't.

- Seek out a mentor and use her, test her, question her, probe her, hug her.

- Be nice to the copy ladies.

- Always remember that first and foremost, these are 12- and 13-year-old kids, and, yes, they honestly do believe that their Friday night plans are much, much more important than proper nouns and Tom Sawyer.

- And I also need to remember that first and foremost, I am still just a 24-year-old person trying to balance my checkbook and send my rent check in on time.

I know what it's like to have the desire to save the world and be the best teacher there ever was. And I know how crushing it is to realize that's not going to happen—at least not the first year. And I know what it's like to cry at school because I'm too overwhelmed and exhausted to deal with grades and attendance slips. And I know what it's like to cry before I go to bed because I can't figure out how to reach that one student. And it was only my first year....

After my first year of teaching, I can say that I have a vision—certainly not an answer or a solution—but a vision nonetheless. I can visualize myself with individualized learning plans, a class full of students all reading different novels, music playing, kids laughing, and behind me will rest full filing cabinets to refer to. I can really see that. But until that vision comes true, I will strive day-to-day to survive, to laugh, to love, to be patient—and to move up from there. And I need to feel safe in the knowledge that is enough for now.

—A summarized excerpt by Tina Humphrey in *Reading Today*, August/September 2000.

The Voice of the Novice Teacher

> **What do you hear in the voice of the seventh- and eighth-grade English teacher summarized above?**
>
> **What can we do better on both sides of the continuum—teacher preparation and the first year of full-time teaching?**

The professional literature resounds with the voices of first-year teachers. Veenman (1984) studied the voices of beginning teachers, defined as teachers who had not yet finished three years of teaching. After analyzing more than 100 empirical studies, Veenman concluded the most serious problems that beginning teachers faced on the job were ranked as follows:

1. Classroom Discipline
2. Motivating Students

3. Dealing with Individual Differences

4. Assessing Student Work

5. Dealing with Parents

6. Organization of Class Work

7. Lack of Materials and Supplies

8. Dealing with Unique Student Problems

9. Heavy Teaching Load

10. Collegial Relationships with Peers

11. Short- and Long-Term Planning of Lessons and Implementation

12. Effective use of Appropriate Teaching Strategies

13. Knowledge of School Policies and Rules

14. Assessing Students' Learning Levels

15. Subject-Matter Knowledge

16. Burden of Nonteaching Assignments

17. Relationships with Principal/Administrative Team

> **How would you rank these problems?**
>
> **What are the most serious risk factors for new teachers at your school or system?**

For beginning teachers the enormous responsibility of the job finally hits home and this feeling is significantly overwhelming when things don't go as planned. Gordon (1991) gives us five environmental factors, presented in Figure 5.1, that confront novice teachers:

Figure 5.1. Beginning Teacher Risk Factors

1. Difficult Work Assignments	Often, beginning teachers start the job with larger classes, more difficult students, and more course preparations than experienced teachers.
2. Unclear Expectations	In addition to the formal expectations cited in faculty handbooks, there are a myriad of informal routines and customs that make up the school culture.
3. Inadequate Resources	First-year teachers lack the stockpile of years of instructional materials, and, often, their classrooms have been stripped of better furniture, materials, and equipment.

| 4. Isolation | Many entry-level teachers view seeking help as an admission of incompetence, and they continually hide serious problems. |
| 5. Reality Shock | The discrepancy between the novice teacher's vision of teaching and the job realties of the situation can cause serious depression, which tends to impact the other factors and make them even more unbearable. |

Each of these factors brings its own set of problems and is intensified when experienced teachers avoid helping new teachers, believing it's not their job or that their advice would be viewed as meddling (Podsen & Denmark, 2000). With new teacher attrition rates of 15 percent and higher for each of the first few years, it seems logical to develop an assistance program to address these issues, especially because it's the most promising teachers who exit the profession. (Gordon, 1991, p. 7). Furthermore, Gordon tells us that those teachers who make it through the first three years often develop a "survival mentality" that negatively impacts on their openness to be reflective and highly skilled teachers.

Characteristics of the Novice Teacher

Adult Development

Traditional novice teachers may be described as young adults ranging in age from 21 to 23. They are very much involved in early adult transition as they leave the more dependent era of preadulthood and begin to take on the responsibilities of a more adult life. Biologically, the 20s and 30s are peak years in the adult life cycle, filled with high energy, high ideals, and lofty goals. It's an era of invincibility, when life is teeming with opportunity, fame, and fortune. However, it is also a time of high stress and anxiety as the young adult takes on additional roles of spouse and parent, and seeks to achieve occupational goals. Internal passions and ambitions drive the young adult from within, and external demands of family, job, community, and society bombard the neophyte from without.

The nontraditional novice teacher comes into teaching from other occupations and brings much in the way of life experiences. Some may be early retirees in their 40s or 50s who come from business and industry, or from the military, and who have many years of productivity ahead. Others "always wanted to be teachers" but were counseled away from education and have decided that helping kids learn is how they now want to spend their remaining work years. Nontraditional inductees in middle adulthood face empty-nest transitions as children mature and leave home. Aging parents also become a factor.

Teacher Development

In contrast to what may be going on with the novice teacher developmentally, the first years of teaching offer a job transition that is often stressful and more complex than the young or older adult ever anticipated. The younger novice teacher searching for status, comfort, and happiness becomes quickly disillusioned as he or she bumps into a workplace beset with obstacles and no help in sight. The older novice teacher, thinking that teaching can't be that difficult and that prior working experiences with adults or with raising their own children will be the same as working with students in classrooms, faces culture shock. In particular, the time demands required for lesson planning and follow-up paperwork outside the teaching day present a work condition that many nontraditional teachers do not expect.

Santrock (2001) reminds us that most of the "difficulty of being a beginning teacher involves the complexity and fast pace of the classroom. Many events are occurring simultaneously and in rapid-fire succession" (p. 6). Researchers have found that teachers may be "involved in as many as 1,000 to 1,500 interactions with students each day" (p. 6). Teachers are continuously making quick decisions to manage both academic and classroom management events in order to keep the instructional time productive.

An area not often considered in the voice of pre-service and first-year teachers encompasses the unique values and beliefs that novice teachers possess about the vision of good teachers that they have developed through personal experience. Kagan (1992) concluded that these beliefs and images of effective teachers, descriptions pre-service teachers have of themselves as teachers, and memories of themselves as students remain static as they sequence their way through teacher preparation and later through teaching internships and in-service teaching. This may also hold true for nontraditional new teachers who have developed established views of education as parents and community members.

According to Steffy et al. (2000, p. 36), "many pre-service teachers assume that the principles of the profession are ideas to prove against the givens of their student-based beliefs (Holt-Reynolds, 1991). Even if their ideas are inadequate, the rationales cannot be discounted because of the central role they play in decision-making and how they define effective teaching." Findings from Kagan's (1992) analysis of 40 studies indicated that novice teachers do not have a clear understanding of the complex interactions between classroom management, behavior, and academic tasks. Novice teachers are very much preoccupied with their own behavior as they attempt to take on the complexities of the job, and this preoccupation may prevent them from focusing on student learning. A quick review of the problems identified by Veenman, described at the beginning of this chapter, seems to confirm this assertion.

Concerned about whether or not pre-service teachers were being prepared with adequate knowledge, skills, and dispositions needed to transition from student teacher to first-year teacher, Meister and Jenks (2000) conducted focus group interviews with 42 nontenured teachers from four states. These participants ranged in age from 21 to 45 years with a mean age of 27 and a mode of 22 years. Twelve were male and 30 were female, with teaching experience ranging from one to three years. The purpose of the study was twofold: (a) To discover common trends that pervade beginning teachers' experiences and (b) To use these trends to better prepare future teachers.

Results of the study yielded several common perceptions that were categorized into three broad themes that concerned beginning teachers: (a) managing behavior and diverse needs of students, (b) dealing with time constraints and workload, and (c) handling conflict with parents and other adults in the school. The researchers concluded that "the three themes form the larger issue that teacher preparation programs need to address. This larger issue is that teaching is filled with moments, often periods, of ambiguity and unpredictability" (p. 9).

Perhaps the most significant finding in the study is the observation that novice teachers do not seem able to easily transfer the knowledge, skills, and attitudes they acquired during teacher preparation and student teaching, particularly when the first- year teaching context was different than the student teaching context. This observation held true if the grade level changed, the content shifted, and if the student behavior varied from well-behaved to more frequent misbehavior. This observation may also support the notion that beginning teachers may be operating at lower levels of conceptual development. They tend to (a) view issues in black and white, (b) have difficulty defining problems they are experiencing, and (c) respond to the same problem in a habitual manner despite the fact that the intervention they are using is not working.

Mesiter & Jenks (2000) indicated that teacher preparation programs may need to (a) emphasize that teaching is not prescriptive but rather unique and personal; (b) encourage risk taking in teaching so novices are not afraid to try new techniques when others don't work; and (c) assist novices in realizing that each teaching context is different, and that their personal belief system of teaching and learning must be monitored and adjusted through systematic self-reflection—not just by trial and error. We strongly believe that site-based mentoring programs should consider these suggestions in their training of mentors.

Career Map 5.1.
Pinpointing the Risk Factors

Based on the information in this chapter, pinpoint the top five risk factors at your school for both traditional novices and alternate-route teachers making a career change. Then brainstorm intervention strategies. Figure 5.2 presents a summary of adult needs and teacher retention risks we presented earlier for traditional and nontraditional inductees:

Figure 5.2. Teacher Inductee: Adult Needs and Retention Risks

Career Stage	Adult Development Needs	Career Retention Risks
Teacher Inductee Traditional 21 to 25	• Modification of relationships with parents and family • Active mastery of the world • Feelings of omnipotence • Search for romance and pursuit of dreams. • Natural inclination toward excitement and idealism	• Realization job is more complex than expected. • Experiencing failure. • Need for acceptance into the teaching community • Need to teach while learning how to teach. • Professional isolation • Facing the risk factors for new teachers without a structured induction/mentoring program
Teacher Inductee Nontraditional	• Will vary depending on age group	• Hasty screening and career assessment processes that do not ensure a best fit between candidate's knowledge, skills, and dispositions for teaching. • Lack of assistance in job transfer of previous knowledge and skills to teaching situation. • Devaluing of previous career experiences and training. • Need to be accepted as an equal partner in the learning process. • Lack of emphasis on experiential learning and problem solving in the teacher preparation training program.

Figure 5.3. What Can We Do to Reduce the Risks for New Teachers?

Risk Factors Traditional Inductees	Current assessment of this risk factor at your school. What are the realities?	Possible Interventions Team Level	Possible Interventions School Level
1			
2			
3			
4			
5			
Risk Factors Alternate Certification Teachers	Current assessment of this risk factor at your school. What are the realities?	Possible Interventions Team Level	Possible Interventions School Level
1			
2			
3			
4			

Minimizing the Risks

Gehrke (1991) argues that teacher development issues need to be more closely linked to the adult lifespan. Acknowledging that adults need to be active agents in their own socialization, Gehrke proposes replacing the culture of professional isolation with professional collaboration. In learning communities, the new teachers would play an active role in selecting their own mentors and peer helpers as individually needed. Levine (1987) contends that professional development for new teachers needs to capitalize on their youthful enthusiasm and idealis. The key is nurturing their need for innovation and adventure and helping them establish and cultivate close collegial relationships that meet their needs for acceptance into the profession (Glickman, 2001).

With teacher shortages increasing across the nation, schools are hiring many divergent types of *new teachers* or *beginning teachers*. Some new teachers come with several years of teaching experience in another state, whereas others are new to the profession but have successfully performed in other careers. Others join the teaching ranks with emergency or provisional licenses, or completion of postbaccalaureate nontraditional pre-service programs.

So what does this mean? It means that new teachers will have various needs and concerns depending on their age, life experiences, and current teacher education profiles. Even though this chapter asks you to center your attention on the needs of beginning teachers, this focus will have to be tempered by the realization that with the varying backgrounds of individuals coming into the profession, nothing is completely predictable. Ganser (1999) emphasizes that "mentoring programs must not assume that the needs of beginning teachers are static." The goal of the induction and mentoring process is, however, to bring the new teacher in as an equal partner in assessing needs and working out individual action plans to address risks perceived by the new teacher and to attempt to eliminate or reduce negative impacts on the inductee.

Career Map 5.2. New Teacher Needs Assessment

Each school context is different; therefore, the needs of your beginning teachers may take on various school profiles. Figure 5.4 presents an inventory to help you in your decision-making process about the needs and concerns facing most new teachers. Review the list and see where you agree or disagree. Revise the list based on the context of your situation and then give it to teachers who are new to your school and beginning teachers as a first step in identifying and prioritizing the areas your induction team may need to study.

Once individual needs have been identified, the next step is to devise ways you can reduce or eliminate these factors within the school. This information can also provide data to help plan staff development support both at the school and system level. Data-driven decision making is useful and essential to making good choices in all areas of school improvement.

Figure 5.4. New Teacher Needs Inventory

Please choose the response for each item that most nearly indicates your level of need for assistance in the area described in the item.

Possible Responses

1. Little need or no need for assistance
2. Some need for assistance
3. Moderate need for assistance
4. High need for assistance
5. Very high need for assistance

Level One: General Orientation and Information Needs

System Information: District Policy and Procedures

_____ Strategic Plan: Goals and Objectives

_____ Teacher Employment and Required Paperwork

_____ Educational Credit Associations

_____ Teacher Supervision and Evaluation System

_____ Personal Leave, Reassignment and Transfer Procedures, Due Process

_____ Job Description, Duties, and Responsibilities

_____ Contracts, Regulations, and Waivers

_____ Teacher Associations and Unions

_____ Professional Insurance

_____ Special Services Provided by the School System

_____ Staff Development Programs

School Information: Policies and Procedures

_____ School Improvement Plan: Goals and Objectives

_____ School Calendar of Important Dates

_____ Teacher Duties and Assignments

_____ Locating and Obtaining Books, Supplies, and Teaching Resources

_____ Student Registration Procedures

_____ Special Education Procedures and Paperwork

_____ Homework Policy

_____ Dress Code

_____ Emergency Procedures (Tornado, Fire, Injuries, Bomb Threat, Intruder Alert)

_____ School Discipline Plan and Process

_____ Substitute Procurement

_____ Teacher Mentoring Program

Team/Grade/Department/Subject Information and Procedures

_____ Team Level Members, Roles, and Responsibilities

_____ Team Grade-Level Planning Periods and Purposes

_____ Administrative Paperwork

_____ Writing Individual Education Plans (IEPs)

_____ Teaming in the Inclusion Classrooms

_____ Team/Grade-Level Classroom Management Plan and Procedures

_____ Curriculum Resources

_____ Communicating with Parents

Level Two: Instruction and Classroom Management Needs

Instructional Needs

_____ Obtaining Instructional Resources/Materials

_____ Writing Lesson Plans

_____ Planning for Instruction

_____ Managing My Time

_____ Diagnosing Student Needs

_____ Assessing and Evaluating Student Progress

_____ Motivating Students

_____ Assisting Students with Special Needs

_____ Understanding the Curriculum

_____ Using a Variety of Teaching Methods

_____ Facilitating Group Discussions

_____ Grouping for Instruction

_____ Cooperative Learning Techniques

_____ Administering Standardized Tests

Classroom Management Needs

_____ Organizing and Managing My Classroom

_____ Establishing a Businesslike Classroom

_____ Maintaining Student Discipline

_____ Establishing Class Rules and Procedures

_____ Enforcing Rules and Consequences Fairly

_____ Teaching Class Rules and Procedures

_____ Helping Students to Monitor Own Behavior and Self-Correct

_____ Minimizing Transitions Between Learning Tasks

_____ Dealing with Aberrant Disruptive Behavior

_____ Dealing with Stress through Conflict Management Techniques

_____ Documenting Student Behavior

Career Map 5.3.
Induction and Mentoring Agenda—
First Six to Nine Weeks

You have had an opportunity to think about how you go about orientating new teachers into your school system and the scope of your induction program. In this chapter, we hitherto explored the prevalent risk factors usually encountered by most beginning teachers and asked you to assess the risk factors you felt needed to be addressed in your school. So how does all of this fit together? Review the induction and mentoring agenda presented in Figure 5.5 for ways we have suggested to induct new teachers in a developmental and sequenced approach that also incorporates strategies for preventing or at least reducing the risks discussed in this section.

Studies of beginning teachers indicate that the initial concern is survival. New teachers want to be successful in gaining the respect of teaching peers and students. They are most concerned about *what is expected* and *how one does things right* in the school community. Their biggest concerns most often center on instructional and classroom management issues. With these points in mind, we think the first six to nine weeks might look like this:

Figure 5.5. Induction and Mentoring Agenda—First Six to Nine Weeks

Orientation to the Setting	Risk Factors	Strategies to Consider
Organizational Policies and Procedures	Need for acceptance and knowing what is expected Professional isolation	*Goal.* The school clearly communicates teacher expectations and norms of teacher conduct and performance. The principal/staff establishes rapport and professional connections with the new staff member. **Strategies** Weekly meetings during the first four to six weeks of school by principal/administrative team to ensure the inductee knows and understands: • System-level and school-level policies, procedures • Teacher evaluation system • School goals and improvement plans for the current school year Weekly meetings during the first 6 to 9 nine weeks by induction/mentoring team to ensure the inductee knows and understands:

		• School-level and team-level curriculum in assigned subject matter • Instructional programs that are currently implemented within the school • Inclusion and special education requirements for meeting the needs of individual students
	Workload Extracurricular duties, multiple preparations, challenging students	*Goal:* **To assess the workload of the inductee to ensure a developmental increase in job duties and responsibilities.** **Strategies** • Eliminate/significantly reduce extra duties and assignments for beginning teachers during the first nine weeks. This means peer teachers will need to pick up the extra assignments during this time. • Develop a timeline covering the first year of when and what duties will be picked up by the beginning teacher for each nine weeks. • Before the new teacher assumes full responsibility for a teaching duty, a system of sharing the assignment for a week or so should be in place to assist in communicating expectations. • Review the class roster of assigned students and ensure that there is not an overload of students with consistent discipline problems. This means peer teachers will need to reassign these students to experienced teachers until the inductee has clearly demonstrated adequate to proficient levels in all areas of classroom management. • Prepare a notebook/computer bank of lesson plans with corresponding activities and assessment tools for the assigned subject(s). This means teachers who have the same teaching assignment might need to formalize their teaching plans so a beginner can implement them.

The challenge of setting up a classroom that is attractive and reflects clear learning goals is important to survival concerns for the new teacher. We suggest focusing mentoring efforts in helping the teacher to quickly establishing a *take-charge, I am the leader,* demeanor starting on the very first day of school. If the new teacher does not take advantage of the first few days of school to make this connection, the chances of it evolving will be difficult to recapture. Experiences in the teacher preparation program have been limited to field experiences where the aspiring teacher has reinforced the management system already in place. The cooperating teacher is always near at hand for resolving difficult discipline problems and classroom management issues. What we need to do is to facilitate the transition from an assisted classroom management role to an independent classroom management role.

For this reason, we strongly urge that the time-consuming task of lesson planning be reduced by allowing the beginner to use lesson plans already developed and tested by experienced peers. The first stage of induction at this point is gaining and maintaining control of the classroom. Once this is clearly established, the new teacher can focus more clearly on instructional tasks.

Figure 5.6. Classroom Management Plan

Classroom Management	Risk Factors	Strategies to Consider
Classroom Organization	Need to teach while learning how to teach. Need to establish a businesslike classroom and orderly work patterns.	*Goal:* **To assist the inductee in designing and implementing a classroom management plan, establishing a positive classroom climate, and organizing the room.** **Strategies** During preplanning the mentor/induction team interviews the new teacher to discuss the following topics: The physical layout of the classroom. • Large group arrangement • Small group areasBulletin boards • Quiet/time-out area • Position of your desk • Organization of materials and supplies • Filing system • Traffic flow • Seating arrangement and seating charts How to handle/record daily routines and student interactions: • Entering the room • Assigning seats • Lunch money and charges • Receipt books • Grade books • Attendance records • Absentee excuses • Plan book • Textbook distribution How to manage student behavior: • Establishing class rules and procedures • Enforcing rules and consequences fairly • Teaching class rules, procedures, and social skills (i.e., team-building, communication, interpersonal, and conflict resolution skills) to build a positive learning community. • Helping students to monitor own behavior and self-correct • Minimizing transitions between learning tasks • Establishing a businesslike climate • Setting reasonable expectations

		• During the first two to four weeks, induction team/mentor should visit each class to monitor the new teacher's classroom management progress. Weekly meetings with new teacher should be scheduled to discuss strengths and growth areas. • During the first two to four weeks, the new teacher should also visit experienced teachers to observe how they have established a businesslike climate. Meetings with these teachers should also take place so the experienced teacher can share thought processes for the decisions made in setting up particular procedures, classroom rules, and student expectations. • If new teacher experiences any classroom management problems, these need to be addressed quickly through problem-solving/reflection-on-action sessions. Remember, the new teacher may have difficulty in transferring knowledge and skills learned in the teacher preparation program. The role of the mentor is to ask the new teacher to assess the situation and develop a plan of attack. • Observing the new teacher's classes during the first six to nine weeks and giving feedback should go a long way in easing the transition and helping the novice become confident and more skillful in managing students. Formative assessment using the INTASC Standards is also suggested.

We think several benefits are achieved by using lesson plans and materials already developed by experienced peers during the first six to nine week. First, the new teacher gets a clear understanding of what the experienced teacher decides is important content and skills that should be taught during this time frame. We know that deciding what to teach and how to teach can be very time-consuming, especially if we are unfamiliar or inexperienced with the subject matter. With current state mandates and emphasis on student testing and achievement, this helps the novice by reducing the stress of wondering if what is being taught is really important. Second, it gives the new teacher an idea of how an experienced teacher teaches the content, modifies it for various learners, and assesses student progress and achievement. Although these aspects have been introduced and practiced in the teacher preparation program, work patterns that reflect best practice have not yet become consistent and internally assimilated.

The research on beginning teachers informs us that novices do not have sufficient dialogue with experienced teachers about why they make the decisions they do. By implementing a reflection-on-action approach early in the mentoring process, new teachers can begin to see how complex teaching really without facing the entire task of both managing the classroom and developing lesson plans at the same time. By asking the new teacher how they would change or modify the lessons, we encourage new teachers to share their ideas, link them to best practice, and develop their lesson resources and teaching style.

Figure 5.7. Classroom Instruction Plan

Classroom Instruction	Risks	Strategies to Consider
	Need to teach while learning how to teach.	**Goal: To assist the new teacher in developing the competencies for a quality teaching performance.**
	Realization job is more complex than expectzzed.	The principal and staff build on the pre-service preparation experiences and help the novice teacher transfer prior knowledge and skills to the new teaching situation.
	Expezriencing failure.	Strategies
		• Prior to each upcoming week, the subject-matter mentor provides lesson plans, materials, and assessment tools.
	Professional isolaztion	• The mentee reviews the materials and completes a work sheet about the lessons provided
	Workload	that addresses these questions:

		• What decisions has the teacher made in developing these lessons? • What do you think is the reason/rationale for the decisions made? • What changes/modifications would you make in teaching these lessons to your students? What is your reason/rationale? • The mentee meets with the subject-matter mentor and reviews these questions. The subject-matter mentor then gives the reasons for the instructional decisions made and reflects with mentee about changes and/or modifications and mentee's reasons. • The mentee visits subject-matter mentor to observe, or even better, to co-teach upcoming lessons. • The assigned mentor visits the mentee's classroom and provides formative feedback on lesson delivery.

Career Map 5.4:
Induction and Mentoring Agenda—
Second Six to Nine Weeks

Once it is evident that the new teacher has a good grasp of classroom management, the remaining six to nine weeks can be planned. Using this framework, plan out how you would sequence the next six to nine weeks. We have made our suggestions in Figure 5.8. We encourage you to add your thoughts and ideas.

Figure 5.8. Induction and Mentoring Agenda—
Second Six to Nine Weeks

Orientation to the Setting	*Risk Factors*	*Strategies to Consider*
Organizational Policies and Procedures	Need for acceptance and knowing what is expected Professional isolation	*Goal:* **The principal/staff/team provides a communication network to build an open forum for presenting problems about the nature of the job.** The principal/staff/team monitors the new teacher for negative attitudes and emotions. **Strategies** • Develop a New Teacher Support Group where novices have a forum that encourages them to discuss problems and share strategies

		• Design an inventory to assess attitudes of beginning teachers at the end of the first semester. • _____ _____ _____
	Workload Extracurricular duties, multiple preparations, challenging students	*Goal:* **To begin to increase the workload of the inductee to ensure a developmental increase in job duties and responsibilities.** To gradually expose new teacher to students who are more difficult to manage. **Strategies** • Based on how the new teacher is performing, begin to implement the gradual increase in job duties and responsibilities with peer support • If possible, give a choice in duties that need to be assumed. • Have the new teacher visit/co-teach with special education teacher or another experienced teacher who manages a group of difficult students well. The purpose here is to expose the novice to students with aberrant behavior and to strategies used by experienced and trained teachers. • Reflective dialogue on decisions made by experienced teachers need to follow these observations. • _____ _____ _____
Classroom Management	*Risk Factors*	*Strategies to Consider*
Classroom Organization	Need to teach while learning how to teach. Need to establish a businesslike classroom and orderly work patterns.	*Goal:* **To assist the inductee in maintaining a positive classroom climate and fostering self-discipline within students as a way to manage student behavior.** **To develop positive home-school communications.** **Strategies** • _____ _____ _____ • _____ _____

		Internet Resource: **Dr. Mac's Amazing Behavior Management Site** offers *Thousands* of tips on managing student behavior, and provides step-by-step directions for implementing a great number of standard interventions. It also has a bulletin board on which you can post your disciplinary concerns and receive suggestions from teachers around the world. http://www.behavioradvisor.com **Burke, Kay, (2000) What to Do With the Kid Who… (Skylight Publisher)** provides current research and step-by-step guidelines/checklists for teaching the social skills, managing conflict, and targeting interventions for students with specific behavior problems. http://www.skylightedu.com
Classroom Instruction	*Risks*	*Strategies to Consider*
	Need to teach while learning how to teach. Realization job is more complex than expected. Professional isolation. Losing enthusiasm and idealistic expectations.	*Goal:* **To assist the new teacher in developing the competencies for a quality teaching performance.** **To encourage new teachers to keep their teaching interesting and exciting through novel approaches to lesson planning and implementation.** **To guide teacher development and nurture collaboration through ongoing mutual professional development and support.** **Strategies** • _____ _____ • _____ _____ **Internet Resources** **TeAch-nology.com** offers teachers *free* access to lesson plans, printable worksheets, over 150,000 reviewedWeb sites, rubrics, educational games, teaching/technology tips, advice from expert teachers, current education news, teacher downloads, teacher finance help, Web quests, and teacher resources for creating just about anything a teacher could need

Summary

Seth's Journal

My mentee is a first-year teacher at the middle school, teaching sixth grade physical science and social studies. She is 24 years old and recently married, and as a result of her marriage, she now has a stepson who is eleven years old. She and her new husband are in the process of building a new home and are interested in starting a family of their own. Needless to say, these additional role responsibilities may present interesting challenges to my mentee. However, she is eager and energetic in her approach toward her new life and her career, and is ready to give it her best shot.

I would place her in the induction stage of teaching. She often debates her decision to enter the teaching profession and voices her concerns about whether or not teaching is the right choice for her. Disillusionment about the job seems to be her hardest struggle right now. Teaching is not what she thought it would be. In the classroom, she wants to be the students' friend, yet is learning to create that line that sets her apart from students. At this time, she does not want to further her education and pursue a Master's Degree. She does, however, wish to participate in professional development programs that will benefit her in her teaching area.

In our meetings together, my mentee has identified classroom management and dealing with parents as her main needs for improvement. In dealing with problems, she does demonstrate the ability to identify specific problems and come up with appropriate solutions. Sometimes, she will just ask me to show her how to do something when she is confused about how to handle a situation or a classroom procedure. This confusion is brief. She is a fast learner and appears able to adapt to a variety of situations within a short time.

References

Feiman-Nemser, S. (2001). Helping novices learn to teach. *Journal of Teacher Education, 52*(1), 17–30.

Gehrke, N. J. (1991). Seeing our way to better helping of beginning teachers. *Educational Forum, 55*(3), 233–242.

Glickman, C. D., Gordon, S., & Ros-Gordon, J. M. (2001). *SuperVision and instructional leadership: A developmental approach.* Needham Heights, MA: Allyn and Bacon.

Gordon, S. P. (1991). *How to help beginning teachers succeed*. Alexandria, VA: Association for Supervision and Curriculum Development.

Holt-Reynolds, D. (1991). *The dialogues of teacher education: Entering and influencing pre-service teachers' internal conversations*. (Research report). East Lansing, MI: National Center for Research on Teacher Learning (ERIC Document Reproduction Service No. ED337459)

Humphrey, T. (2000, August/September). Knowing enough for now. *Reading Today*, p. 4.

Kagan, D. M. (1992). Professional growth among pre-service and beginning teachers. *Review of Educational Research, 62*(2), 129–169.

Levine, S. L. (1987). Understanding life cycle issues: A resource for school leaders. *Journal of Education, 169*(1), 7–19.

Meister, D. G., & Jenks, C. (2000). Making the transition from pre-service to in-service teaching: Beginning teachers' reflections. *Journal of the Association of Teacher Educators, 22*(3), 1–11.

National Foundation for Improvement in Education. (1999, February). *Creating a teacher mentoring program*. Proceedings of the NFIE Teacher Mentoring Symposium, Los Angeles, CA. Available from: http://www.nfie.org/publications/ mentoring.htm. Retrieved 5/20/01.

Podsen, I. J., & Denmark, V. (2000). *Coaching and mentoring first-year and student teachers*. Larchmont, NY: Eye On Education.

Santrock, J. (2001). *Educational psychology*. New York: McGraw-Hill Higher Education.

Steffey, B. E., Wolfe, M. P., Pasch, S. H., and Enz, B. J. (Eds.). (2000). *Life cycle of the career teacher*. Thousand Oaks, CA: Corwin Press

Veenman, S. (1984). Perceived problems of beginning teachers. *Review of Educational Research, 54*(2), 143–178.

6

Mentoring:
Doing the Right Thing

The mere presence of a mentor is not enough; the mentor's knowledge of how to support a new teacher and skill at providing guidance are also crucial.

Holloway J., 2001

Why Mentor?

For many first year teachers, teaching becomes a journey for which there is no map to guide them. Kenneth Wilson (1999), a Nobel-laureaute physicist at Ohio State University and a member of the National Foundation for the Improvement in Education, makes this analogy: Imagine that you aspire to be a mountain climber. You have the necessary equipment and endless energy and enthusiasm, but you have never even climbed a tree all the way to the top. There are several ways to approach the task. You could take a practice run with an experienced mountaineer willing to show you the ropes or you could be taken to the base of the mountain, dropped off, and told to get to the top or quit. Given these choices, which approach would you select?

We know teacher mentoring has been around for a long time, but it has existed more informally. According to researchers (Jones & Jambor, 1996), there are three unspoken proverbs for new teachers coming into the profession. *"Figure it out for yourself. Do it yourself. Keep it to yourself."* Too often, beginning teachers find themselves alone at the bottom of the world's tallest mountain. So what can we do to keep talented beginners in the classroom for the long climb to the top of their teaching career?

The focal point of any induction system is the teacher-mentoring component. Teacher mentoring has been around for a long time, but has existed in more informal and unsystematic formats. The need for a structured mentoring system is essential if schools are going to attract and retain qualified teachers. Informal mentoring is not enough to support beginning teachers and teachers new to the school. In order to ensure that every new teacher has the same opportunity to be successful in the job assigned, a structured mentoring program needs to be in place.

Sweeney (1999) gives us several reasons why informal mentoring will not help us retain and develop talented teachers:

♦ New teachers do not find it easy to ask for help.

♦ Building for transfer of newly acquired knowledge and best practices during the pre-service program must be systematically supported and encouraged at the school site by trained mentors

♦ Experienced teachers are reluctant to intrude into another teacher's classroom.

♦ Informal mentors are not provided mentor training and therefore do not clearly understand their role and tasks.

♦ Informal mentoring is not supported, recognized, and rewarded.

♦ Informal mentoring provides no assurance that all new staff members are being assisted and their needs are being addressed.

"Increasingly, school districts are working with teacher associations, universities, and others to establish mentoring programs to help beginning teachers, veteran teachers in new assignments, and teachers in need of remedial aid to build up to the difficult climbs with the assistance of a guide. The hope is that in due time the profession as a whole will be able to tackle the Everests of the educational landscape." (NFIE, 1999, p. 2)

> **What purpose does teacher mentoring serve in your school and school district?**
> **What training is provided to your teacher mentors?**
> **How supportive are you of the process and the needs of both new teacher and their mentors?**

Purposes for Mentoring

Sweeny (1998) tells us that "mentoring purposes vary from orientation, to induction, to instructional improvement, to an intent to change the culture of the school to a more collaborative learning environment." What purposes will drive your mentoring program? Will teacher mentoring focus on: (a) assisting mentees to speed up the learning of a new job or skill and reduce the stress of transition; (b) improving instructional performance of novices through modeling and cognitive coaching by a top performer; or (c) socialization of mentees into the profession of teaching. You must decide—depending upon the age, experience, and skills of the student intern, beginner teacher, or experienced teacher—as to which purpose will take precedence.

Perhaps the best reason to mentor new teachers is to model collaborative learning and professional growth. We have to make changes in the educational landscape by shifting from a culture of *doing it alone to doing it together* and finding ways to make it happen. Little (1996) tells us that outstanding schools "organize teachers' work in ways that demonstrably reduce teacher isolation and enhance opportunities for teacher learning, both inside and outside the school (p. 1). Our history of professional isolation may be one of the key factors in losing new teachers. Left alone to figure out the complex interactions embedded in teaching for themselves, they experience more failures than successes, lose their confidence and enthusiasm, and, finally, quit.

Lieberman (2000) states that "teacher development has been limited by a lack of knowledge of how teachers learn (p. 8). Studies of first-year teachers and reflections of mentor teachers are beginning to inform the knowledge base (Boyer, 1999; Evertson & Smithey, 1999). Preparing aspiring teachers for the complex and multifaceted profession of teaching continues to challenge pre-service teacher education. Ethell & McMeniman (2000) assert that despite the commitment of teacher education institutions to provide effective pre-service training, research shows that student teachers engage in field experiences and internships where they model teaching practice on the observable behaviors of the supervising/cooperating teachers but do not have a clear understanding of the cognitive world of the expert practitioner.

Furthermore, they indicate that student teachers often fail to build on the learning and understanding from their coursework, perceiving much of it as irrelevant or merely the means to get through the course. These researchers conclude that pre-service programs may need to develop intervention strategies that ask the novice to not only observe and model effective teaching behaviors, but also to be able to identify and articulate the intentions underlying expert teachers' practice.

Schon (1987) reinforces this notion. His knowing-in-action model rejects the separation of theory and practice and argues for ongoing reflective and collaborative discussion between, and among, those involved in teaching and learning. Schon directs attention to the practitioner's ability to engage in reflection-in-action (the ability to revise constructs of teaching and learning while engaged in practice) and reflection-on-action (the ability to think back over practice in a systematic way). The knowledge base on reflective practice should be an important aspect in training teacher mentors if we are to truly help the novice in understanding the complexity of teaching and learning.

> What can principals and instructional lead teachers do to support teacher mentoring?
>
> How can principals structure inquiry groups so novice teachers could hear expert teachers explain rationale for teaching decisions and link teaching behaviors to best practice?

Benefits of Mentoring

Teacher Retention

The National Center for Education Statistics reports that 9.3 percent of new teachers leave the profession after only one year (1994–95). An additional 11.1 percent leave their assignments for teaching positions elsewhere after their first year. In rural areas and inner cities, these rates are often higher. Overall, mentoring new teachers has clearly demonstrated that this approach helps to keep talented teachers on the job (National Association of State Boards of Education, 1998). Research studies examining the impact of mentoring programs all show high retention rates for new teachers (DeBolt, 1991; Boyer, 1999). Here are two examples:

Montana Beginning Teacher Support Program (1997)

- 97 percent of mentored teachers remained in the profession after the first year.

- 91 percent of the mentored teachers were still in the profession after three years.

Texas A & M University-Corpus Christie Induction Program (1995)

- 94 percent of mentored teacher remained in the classroom compared to the nationwide trend of 50 percent attrition.

Effective teacher mentoring can eliminate, or significantly reduce, the number of problems faced by beginning teachers. School systems and university teacher education programs involved in team approaches to teacher induction find that novices show significantly better performance and more positive attitudes and perceptions about teaching than those not involved in some type of structured mentoring program (Henry, 1988). Gordon (1991) reports that beginning teachers indicated that their peer mentors provided help in such areas as location of instructional materials, classroom management, lesson planning, assessing and grading students, establishing realistic expectations of student work and behavior, and having someone to talk to and listen to their concerns. This assistance addresses many of the risk factors that often lead first-year teachers to leave the profession.

Teaching Effectiveness

According to the National Foundation for the Improvement of Education (NFIE, 1999), there is consistent evidence that mentoring improves the quality of teaching. "In its January 1999 Teacher Quality study, the National Center for Education Statistics reports that seven in ten teachers who receive mentoring at least once a week believe that their instructional skills have improved 'a lot' as result" (p. 4). In addition, the majority of the mentors also reported significant improvements to their own teaching skills.

In a fully developed teacher-mentoring program, master teachers get the opportunity to emerge from their isolated classrooms and see what's going on in their schools and even in their school district. The specialized mentor training provides an infusion of new knowledge and skills, which often revitalizes one's personal and professional growth. One ex-mentor commented, "After serving as a peer mentor last year, I returned to my classroom with a refreshed and renewed attitude. Being away from the classroom and working with first-year teachers helped me to reflect on what I did as a teacher and why. This reflection led to better ideas and the creation of a more positive learning situation for my students this year." Overall, both cooperating teachers and peer mentors report the process is beneficial to them, saying it helped them to grow professionally, to develop a clearer idea of effective teaching, and to understand the importance of effective interaction and collaboration skills (Hawk 1987; Odell, 1990).

Similarly, according to Holloway (2000), in reporting the impact of the California Formative Assessment and Support System for Teachers, "…mentoring played a significant role in professional growth of new teachers. Specifically the program's design helped new teachers hone their practice—planning lessons, for example—and reflect on the effectives of their instruction. Mentors also found that working with beginning teachers engaged them in reflection about their own instructional practices" (pp. 85–86).

Learning Community

Teacher mentoring is not the answer to all of the problems in teacher retention, and individual mentors cannot do all the work. Support is needed from all aspects of the school community to make this program work for all involved. Experts in teacher mentoring strongly urge school faculties to engage in conversations about how best to induct new colleagues into the workplace. Experienced faculty need to assume a leadership role by taking on the more challenging students, providing model lesson plans and resources, reducing the number of class preparations, team teaching, and modeling collaboration and team work. "Mentoring becomes inseparable from the daily business of a school and helps to create an ethos of life long learning. Every faculty member acquires an important role to play, however indirectly, by contributing to a school climate that fosters assistance for new and veteran teachers alike" (NFIE, 1999, p. 7).

Key Components of Mentoring Programs

Figure 6.1 presents several key components of teacher mentoring programs found in the professional literature. Compare your program to see how many components you have included and what areas you might consider in the future.

Career Map 6.1.
Analyzing Your Teacher Mentoring Program

Figure 6.1. Existing Mentoring Program Checklist

Components	Yes	Evidence	No	Why Needed
Structured Mentoring System				
• Purposes for mentoring clearly defined and communicated to all stakeholders				
• Clear standards for beginning teachers linked to local/state/national guidelines for teaching and learning				
• Focuses on improving practice				
• Clear selection criteria for mentors				

• Structured training program for mentors
  • Well-articulated roles and tasks for mentors and mentees
  • Knowledge base and performance competencies for mentors clearly defined and assessed.				

• Planned staff development activities to support mentoring program				
• Mentor support groups for problem solving and professional development				
• Reduces the workloads for beginning teachers and mentors.				
• Compensation and rewards for mentors is provided.				
• Extends beyond the first year of a teacher's career				
• Program evaluation relating to goals and objectives of the mentoring program.				

Mentor's Roles and Tasks

Learning to be a good mentor and doing mentoring takes time. Mentors need to be patient with themselves and the process. Finding the time in already busy schedules will always be a factor. **Having a supportive principal is generally the key to how successful any program will be at the school level.**

The most difficult part of the process for mentors, is knowing what the mentoring role means. Sweeny (1994) points out that "the role must be well-defined, especially if you have expectations for results." If the mentor thinks of him/herself as *a teacher coach* or a *support teacher,* he/she begins to define the role in terms of function. Once the role becomes clear, then the mentoring tasks also become more evident. As a *teacher coach,* the mentor might be involved in activities of observing performance, questioning the rationale for selected teaching behaviors, providing feedback for self-correction if needed, and modeling best practice. As a *support teacher,* the mentor might be involved as a buddy, targeted to be available should questions or concerns arise.

Mentor teachers can't do it all. Part of the role will necessitate helping mentees assess performance areas that are most critical for them. Mentors will need a sound understanding of the current frameworks for effective teaching in order to help novices diagnose both strengths and growth targets and a will also need a discerning eye to judge when the novices are ready to learn more complex teaching behaviors. The relationship between mentors and mentees needs to be collaborative. To facilitate this relationship, mentors must know their own strengths and weaknesses and be open to learning and working in partnership with college personnel and school colleagues.

> **How are mentors selected and assigned to new teachers in your school? Do you seek input from both mentors and mentees about how these partnerships might be formed?**
>
> **What are the advantages to you and the school in developing a selection and matching process?**

Selection of Mentors

How are mentors selected? Most teacher preparation programs work with building-level administrators in outlining the qualities they seek in a cooperating teacher or first-year mentor teacher. The final choice rests with the building principal. As collaborative partnerships develop through professional development schools, the selection of mentors is evolving from "who's ready, willing, and able" to "what experienced teacher is a best qualified and a good match for a particular intern or entry-level teacher."

The literature base on mentoring purports that there are two approaches in selecting mentors: exclusive or inclusive. Exclusive approaches limit the choice to the best models of excellent instruction, rejecting other experienced teachers as "not good enough." The risks of these approaches include developing an "elite group" and perhaps overemphasizing the technical skills of teachers. Mentoring in this approach may cause more divisive behaviors as teachers vie for this status. Stress levels for all concerned also tend to increase if mentor teachers see the success of interns reflecting on their teaching status.

Inclusive approaches seek to select as best models those teachers who are continual, life-long learners. Approaches like this offer all veteran teachers the opportunity to be mentors, giving them the option to self-select out if, and when, the mentoring role becomes uncomfortable. Analogous to the thinking that sometimes the best teachers don't always become effective administrators, we know that some effective teachers do not always have the characteristics to be effective mentors. The mentor's role in this approach is to model professional growth, focus on improving the novice's teaching, and to support the novice during the process. Interpersonal and cognitive coaching skills are highly valued as a more learner-centered approach to the mentoring process is fostered.

Overall selection processes for qualified mentors are varied, depending on the conditions of supply and demand within the school. Some school systems have a rigorous process for selecting mentors that may include such steps as: (a) nomination of candidates, (b) letters of recommendation, (c) required number of years of experience, (d) review by a school panel, and (e) Critique of a teaching episode and written suggestions for review by the school panel. Other school systems, where there are more new teachers and a dwindling number of experienced teachers, are experimenting with a team approach to mentoring. The new teacher is matched to several different mentors who in turn offer assistance in various specialized areas depending on the needs of the mentee.

Mentor Qualifications

What does it take to be a good mentor? Gordon (1991) summarizes the research based on effective mentors and concluded that the "most important characteristic of a successful mentor is a commitment to provide personal time and attention to the beginner" (p. 30). Nothing can be more demoralizing than a peer mentor scurrying around, implying through body language and actions that he or she is too busy to set aside the time needed to focus on the novice. Effective mentors demonstrate a variety of skills and knowledge that come with experience. They are very familiar with policies and procedures within the school system and their local schools, and they know how to navigate among the stakeholders. They possess political savvy and have access to a network of administrative and instructional resources. Effective mentors have good people and communication skills.

Figure 6.2 presents a checklist we have devised that reflects the qualities thought to be desired for effective mentors.

Career Map 6.2. Mentor Qualfications Checklist

Figure 6.2. Characteristics of Successful Mentors

Characteristics of Successful Mentors	High	Moderate	Low
Professional Demeanor			
Willingness to set aside time for mentee development			
Willing to be trained in mentoring			
Wide range of interests			
Positive view of people and teaching profession			
Confident in professional and personal realms			
Dependable and trustworthy			
Believes mentoring improves practice			
Feels comfortable observing peers			
Enjoys challenges and solving problems			
Competence and Experience			
Track record of high professional achievement			
Ability to work with adults as well as students			
Open to new ideas			
Adaptable in new situations			
Able to maneuver within, and show influence in, the system.			
Viewed by peers as professional and competent			
Highly skilled as a teacher in instructional skills and classroom management			
Communication Skills			
Good listener			
Demonstrates reflective questioning skills and approaches			
Can make a clear presentation of ideas			
Provides feedback in nonjudgmental ways			
Maintains confidentiality within the mentoring role			
Interpersonal Skills			
Congenial, accessible, and user-friendly			
Genuine and sincere in helping others			
Inspires enthusiasm , hope and optimism			
Patient, helpful, and caring			
Collaborates well with colleagues			
Develops positive working relationship with novices			

Support for Mentoring in Schools

Mentors need ongoing organizational and technical backing. Regularly scheduled seminars for mentors are suggested as a way to provide mutual support and assistance, so mentors can share problems and successful strategies for mentoring novices. Mentors also require released time to plan support activities, observe novices, dialogue and reflect about practice, provide feedback, gather instructional resources, and team-teach lessons to demonstrate effective teaching approaches. For first-year peer mentors in particular, "the addition of these responsibilities onto an already hectic work schedule is a disservice to the mentor and will significantly impact the quality of support to the first-year teacher" (Gordon, 1991, p. 38). Here are several ways to support mentors:

- ♦ Substitute time in order to mentor. Sweeny (1994) recommends one day per month used in half-day blocks.

- ♦ Incentives for mentors such as: release time from supervision duty, opportunity to attend a conference or workshop with the mentee, reduced number of teaching classes, tuition for graduate work targeted for mentor training, and some form of formal recognition through merit pay, certificates, and plaques.

- ♦ Formal recognition of the contributions made by both cooperating teacher and peer mentors.

Rowley (1999) reinforces this notion by asserting that "although the majority of mentor teachers would do this important work without compensation, we must not overlook the relationship between compensation and commitment. Programs that provide mentors with a stipend, release time from extra duties, or additional opportunities for professional growth, make important statements about the value of the work and its significance in the school community" (p. 20).

> What resources are available to you to support mentoring?
>
> How can you alter the school workday to build in the time for mentors to work with their mentees?
>
> What support do you need from the system level.

The Importance of Mentor Training

The importance of training mentors cannot be overlooked (Kyle, D., Moore, G., & Sanders, J., 1999). Teachers and school administrators involved in sustained and effective programs emphasize that training for mentors needs to be ongoing. Some programs provide mentors with opportunities to collaborate with local universities. These programs share ideas about effective mentoring strategies to bridge the gap between pre-service and in-service experiences. Other programs structure mentor support groups within schools or at the district level, so mentors can share problems, discuss coaching strategies, and plan ways to meet the needs of their mentees.

Effective mentoring programs clearly define the knowledge and skills experienced teachers need to acquire if they are to be successful mentors. Given the conclusion that informal mentoring is not enough to get the job done, veteran teachers need specific program preparation if they are to approach the mentoring role confidently and competently. The Missouri training model (NFIE, 1999) for mentors includes training assistance in the following areas:

♦ Facilitating reflective practice

♦ Understanding state mandates

♦ Establishing collaborative relationships based on trust, collegiality, and confidentiality

♦ Developing classroom observation skills

♦ Creating long-term professional development plans

♦ Understanding the academic, professional, and social needs of new teachers

Podsen and Denmark (2000) affirm that the ability of a mentor to function skillfully in meeting the purposes of the teacher-mentoring program will increase success, if clearly defined program content and performances are targeted. They present eight competencies that should be considered in a training program for aspiring mentors:

1. Know the Mentoring Role and Tasks
2. Promote Collaborative Learning and Professional Community
3. Nurture the Novice Based on Adult Learning Needs
4. Develop Performance and Cognitive Coaching Skills
5. Model and Coach Effective Teaching Based on National Standards
6. Model and Coach Effective Classroom Management Based on National Standards
7. Display Sensitivity to Individual Differences Among Learners
8. Demonstrate the Willingness to Assume a Redefined Professional Role as a Teacher Leader

Gordon (1991) points out that "the single greatest problem in mentoring programs that aren't functioning well is the lack of mentor preparation" (p. 31). For all new teachers to receive consistent and equitable support, we need to ensure that the mentors know their role and can demonstrate the skills required within the mentoring process.

Measuring Program Effectiveness

Effective programs involve a cycle of planning, implementing, assessing results, and using such results to renew planning for improvement. Peer mentors need to seek information about their mentoring skills and the impact of mentoring on mentees. Specifically, what is the impact of the mentoring program on retention, the quality of the teaching performance, and, ultimately, the impact on student achievement. Do we have evidence to show that first-year teachers feel more confident and capable and therefore remain in teaching? Is there an increase in content knowledge and pedagogical skills based on clear standards and benchmarks? Do mentored teachers show fewer problems with classroom management, maintain a positive attitude about the profession, and seek out professional growth? Does classroom student assessment data show how the new teacher has had a positive impact on student learning?

School systems and teacher preparation programs need to seek data about the effects of teacher mentoring in their respective school districts or teacher education programs. Such program evaluation could yield valuable data and suggest alternative approaches to improve teacher mentoring and pre-service programs. Evaluation and careful documentation accomplish two goals: (a) they provide feedback for program improvement and (b) they justify the cost to decision makers and education stakeholders.

On a broader scale, "does the cost of mentoring programs offer a significant return on the investment—that the cost of mentoring and retaining new teachers is less than the combined outlay for large-scale recruitment and long-term remediation" (NFIE, 1999, p. 16). This would seem to be a crucial question for school systems to investigate.

Career Map 6.3. Program Evaluation

Figure 6.3. Sample Mentoring Program End-of-Year Survey

For each item, please indicate the response that best describes your opinion about the assistance you received in the mentoring program. The purpose of this survey is to improve our program. Please do not write your name or school on this survey.

Please rate the assistance provided by your mentor teacher in these areas:

1. Not very helpful.
2. Some help was provided.
3. Help was consistently provided and useful.
4. Help was planned based on my needs. Very Helpful
5. Help was planned, provided, and had a significant impact on my teaching performance. Exceptionally Helpful.

General Information	1	2	3	4	5
• Orientation to the school system					
• Orientation to the school facilities					
• Orientation to the curriculum/instructional program					
Job-Specific Information					
• Becoming acquainted with the school staff and learning how things work in this school.					
• Becoming acquainted with the students and the general characteristics of the school community					
• Setting up my room and organizing for the first week of school					
• Locating or providing materials and resources					
• Planning instruction					
• Providing assistance in developing my teaching strategies					
• Providing information or assistance with classroom management and/or school discipline policies					
• Providing information and assistance about required paperwork					
Coaching and Mentoring Support					
• Observing and giving feedback on my teaching					
• Promoting my ability to think about my practice					

• Collaborating with me as a professional to assess my performance, develop goals, and implement action plans				
• Being available when I needed assistance				
• Listening supportively to my questions and concerns				
• Establishing a schedule of regular meeting times to address needs and concerns				

Please respond to these questions so we can improve our mentoring program. As a teacher new to your school, what needs, problems or concerns did you experience in your first weeks of teaching?

How would you describe the assistance and support you received from the principal/assistant principal?

Please list or describe the most important or useful support provided you by your mentor teacher or you school's Teacher Induction Team.

Please suggest ways in which a teacher new to a school might be better supported throughout the first years of teaching.

Do you intend to return to teaching next year? _____ Yes _____ No
If *No*, please give your primary reason for leaving.

If *Yes*, please give your primary reason for staying with us.

Summary

To end this chapter are the following reflections of teacher leaders who were trained as teacher mentors within the education specialist program for teacher leaders. These leaders coached beginning teachers and teachers new to their schools during their mentoring internship.

Becky's Journal

My mentee is excited about having me as a mentor. We have worked together for one full year now. She has consulted me often, and we share many materials, ideas, and concerns. I have the Special Education Management System on my computer, and I work collaboratively with my mentee in helping her to write her IEPs. After my mentee completed the needs assessment, I carefully reviewed the results to determine which areas she felt she needed the most assistance with. Together we worked on a plan to meet her needs. . . .It is my desire to use what I know about me mentee to help her foster the confidence she needs to make independent decisions, to develop an intact self-confidence, to focus more intensely on lessons that actively involve student participation, and to begin to think of herself as the highly competent, capable, and dedicated educator that she is quickly becoming.

I feel I should always lead by example; therefore, as a mentor, I strive to exhibit the best habits and behaviors associated with cognitive teaching. To this end, I have guided my mentee through two meaningful and productive cognitive coaching cycles. I have also encouraged my mentee to participate in professional organizations, such as the Council for Exceptional Children, so that she can be regularly informed of new practices, ideas, and strategies in educating special education students. . . .

As a new mentor, I worked hard to provide appropriate literature and suggestions for best practice, modeled desirable teaching behaviors, provided opportunities for joint reflection and self-reflection of teaching performance, and engaged in a highly organized and committed coaching process. I feel that my mentee and I have demonstrated a successful mentoring process that has resulted in two more significantly confident, competent, and knowledgeable educators—my mentee and myself. As a teacher leader, mentoring has proven to be a tremendous and positive growth experience for me.

Tim's Journal

I find it interesting that support of mentoring, particularly providing mentors release time, has been identified as a critical component of the induction process. Release time involves a reduced workload to allow time for the mentor to observe and conference together about teaching. At the system level, this seems to be the least area of concern.

Michelle's Journal

With less than five years of teaching experience under my belt, I am shocked at the percentage of teacher "drop-outs" that occur within the first five years of teaching. My first year of teaching was successful because of a mentor. I think mentoring programs should be required in all states to help new teachers through the difficult first year, as well as help veteran teachers reflect and gain a sense of renewal about their profession.

Jon's Journal

I was saddened to realize that my school system lacks many of the key components associated with successful mentoring programs. I cannot help but think that our mentoring program is doomed to fail. The main weaknesses are the lack of time for the mentor to interact with the entry-level teacher, no financial support for the program, and no system of program evaluation to determine the impact of the program on new teachers.

Melanie's Journal

Teaching, at any stage of the game, can be an isolating, and sometimes thankless profession. Having a person to discuss your day with and give you advice is a very valuable thing. Most beginning teachers would welcome this opportunity.

Carolyn's Journal

The thing that has surprised me the most is how much I have benefited from being a mentor. I have improved my own classroom skills through the mentoring training program and become more aware of the needs of new teachers. As a result of mentoring a new teacher, I am more enthusiastic and energetic about my work. I feel that I have made a difference in keeping a colleague in the profession.

References

Boyer, K. (1999). *A qualitative analysis of the impact of mentorships on new special education educators' decision to remain in the field of special education.* Unpublished doctoral dissertation, George Mason University, Fairfax, VA.

DeBolt, G. (1991). *Mentoring: Studies of effective programs in education*. Paper presented at the Diversity in Mentoring Conference, Chicago, IL. (ERIC Document Reproduction Services No. ED346166)

Denmark, V., & Podsen, I. J. (2000). The mettle of a mentor. *Journal of Staff Development, 21*(4),18–22.

Ethell, R. G., & McMeniman, M. (2000, March-April). Unlocking the knowledge in action of an expert practitioner. *Journal of Teacher Education, 51*(2), 87–101.

Evertson, C., & Smithey, M. (2000). Mentoring effects on protégés' classroom practice: An experimental field study. *Journal of Educational Research, 93*(5), 294–304.

Gordon, S. (1991). *How to help beginning teachers succeed*. Alexandria, VA: Association for Supervision and Curriculum Development.

Hawk, P. (1987). Beginning teacher programs: Benefits for the experienced educator. *Action in Teacher Education, 8*(4), 59–63.

Henry, M. A. (1988). *Project credit: Certification renewal experiences designed to improve teaching*. Indiana State University at Terre Haute, Department of Secondary Education. (ERIC Document Reproduction Service No. ED291681)

Holloway, J. (2001). The benefits of mentoring. *Educational Leadership, 58*(8), 85–86 Alexandria, VA: Association for Supervision and Curriculum Development.

Jones, R., & Jambor, M. (1996). *Reforming education one classroom at a time: A guide for developing an intensive mentoring program*. Birmingham, AL: Jefferson County Board of Education.

Kyle, D., Moore, G., & Sanders, J. (1999). The role of the mentor teacher: Insights, challenges, and implications. *Peabody Journal of Education, 74*(3–4), 109–122.

Lieberman, A. (2000). *Practices that support teacher development: Transforming conceptions of professional development*. National Center for Restructuring Education, Schools, and Teaching. Available from: http://www.her.nsf.gov/HER/REC/pubs/NSF_EF/lieber.htm

Little, J. W. (1996). *Excellence in professional development and professional community*. Northwest Regional Educational Laboratory: School Improvement Program: National Specialty in School Change. Available from: http://www.nwrel.org/scpd/natspec/excellence.html

National Association of State Boards of Education. (1998). *The numbers game.* Alexandria, VA: Author.

National Center for Education Statistics (NCES). (1997). *Condition of education.* Available from: http://nces.ed.gov/nces/pubs/ce/c970d01.htlm

National Foundation for Improvement in Education (1999, February). *Creating a teacher mentoring program.* Proceedings of the NFIE Teacher Mentoring Symposium. Available from: http://www.nfie.org/publications/mentoring.htm

Odell, S. J. (1990). A collaborative approach to teacher induction that works. *The Journal of Staff Development, 11*(4), 12–16.

Podsen, I. J., & Denmark, V. (2000). *Coaching and mentoring first-year and student teachers.* Larchmont, NY: Eye On Education.

Rowley, J. (1999). The good mentor. *Educational Leadership, 56*(8), 20–22.

Schon, D. (1987). *Educating the reflective practitioner: Toward a new design for teaching and learning in the profession.* San Francisco: Jossey-Bass.

Spuhler, L., & Zetler, A. (1995). *Montana beginning teacher support program. Research report for year three 1994–95.* Helena, MT: Montana State Board of Education. (ERIC Document Reproduction Service No. ED3900803)

Sweeny, B. (1999). *Mentoring to improve schools.* Alexandria, VA: Association for Supervision and Curriculum Development.

Sweeny, B. (1998). *What's happening in mentoring and induction in each of the United States?* MLRN Mentoring Library. Available from: http://www.teachermentors.com & http://www.mentors.net

Sweeny, B. (1994, Spring). A new teacher mentoring knowledge base of best practices: A summary of lessons learned from practitioners. *MLRN Mentoring Library, 3*(2). Available from: http://www.teachermentors.com

Sweeny, B. (1992, Winter). Advice to beginning mentors. *MLRN Mentoring Library,1*(1). Available from: http://www.teachermentors.com

Teacher Inductee:
Mentoring Resources and Internet Tools

Brzoska, T., Jones. J., Mahaffey, J., Miller, J. K., & Mychats, J. (1987). *Mentor teacher handbook.* Portland, OR: Northwest Regional Educational Laboratory. (ERIC Document Reproduction Service No. 288 820)

Gordon, S. P., & Maxey, S. (2000). *How to help beginning teachers succeed* (2nd ed.). Alexandria, VA: Association for Supervision and Curriculum Development.

Moir, E. (1990). *Phases of first year teaching*. Sacramento, CA: California Department of Education. Available from: http://newteachercenter.org/article3.html.

National Foundation for the Improvement of Education. (1999). *Creating a teacher mentoring program*. Washington, D.C.: Author. Available from: http://nfie.org/publications/mentoring.htm.

Podsen, I., & Denmark, V. (2000). *Coaching and mentoring first-year and student teachers*. Larchmont, NY: Eye On Education.

Podsen I., & Krause, B. (in press, available March 2002). *The teacher mentor training guide*. Gainesville, GA: Mindscapes Publishing. E-mail: mindscp55@aol.com. This training guide provides school systems with a systematic training format designed to help staff developers train teacher mentors in their schools. The guide presents training scripts, activities, overheads, handouts, forms, and training resources for fifteen competency modules focusing on key mentoring tasks, knowledge, and skills.

7

Implications for Continuous Professional Learning

Unless you try to do something beyond what you have already mastered, you will never grow.

Ronald E. Osborn,
Great Quotations

How can we go about setting the framework for a teaching career based on the premise that lifelong learning is not an option? It is essential! Carr and Harris (2001) tell us that continuous adult learning plays an important and primary role in improving students' learning. They assert that "in a standards-based environment, adult needs, goals, and satisfaction are no longer the center of professional development" (p. 123). In fact, they conclude that over the teaching career—professional development, supervision, and evaluation must center on the improvement of student learning in relation to standards.

However, we would temper this approach by suggesting that adult learning needs and individual professional aspirations should be considered in equal partnership with the needs and school improvement goals of the district. We believe that professional development, supervision, and evaluation must center on both the improvement of student learning and teacher learning. The professional learning goals of the teacher must be considered if teacher self-actualization and efficacy are to be valued. Sparks and Loucks-Horsley (1989) assert that "self-directed development empowers teachers to address their own problems and by doing so, creates a sense of professionalism" (p. 1).

> What views of professional development guide teacher development in your school or school system?
>
> Have you ever asked why we need to require teachers to take 5 to 10 hours of staff development in order to keep their certification current?

> What if all our teachers were expected to be self-directed and set their own professional goals. How would this approach affect our current staff development views?

Most would agree that most school districts support teachers' investment in their professional knowledge and skills. Districts sponsor classes and workshops, and teachers work on advanced certificates or degrees, and attend professional conferences and summer institutes. However, "these efforts often have little impact on student learning because they tend to be disjointed, unfocused, and offer teachers few opportunities to learn by doing and reflecting on practice with their colleagues. In other words, professional development frequently lacks connection to practice and to high standards of student achievement or teacher development" (Promising Practices, 1998. p. 1).

Guidelines to Consider

Loucks-Horsley (1998), in collaboration with peers, specifies seven key guidelines for designing effective teacher development approaches. Effective professional development experiences target these aspects:

1. Operate based on a clear vision of teaching and learning
2. Provide teachers opportunities to build their knowledge and skills
3. Use and model the strategies teachers are to use with students
4. Build a learning community
5. Support teachers to serve in leadership roles
6. Create links to all parts of the educational system
7. Assess and monitor both teacher growth and student improvement

Likewise, Guskey (1995) offers six guidelines for designing a successful professional development approach. He suggests that effective professional development experiences accomplish the following:

1. Target growth as both an individual and an organizational process
2. Have a grand plan but start small
3. Work in support teams
4. Include standards and benchmarks for feedback focus
5. Provide follow-up, support, evidence of impact
6. Integrate individual plans with school improvement goals

Professional Development Approach for Teacher Inductees

Using the guiding principles suggested above, we outline a seven-step professional development approach that addresses the needs of the Teacher Inductee.

Step 1: Set High Expectations Based on National Standards for Effective Teaching And Learning

Beginning in the pre-service program, the development of a clear vision of teaching and learning begins. Most teacher education programs have linked their conceptual frameworks to the Interstate New Teachers Assessment Consortium Standards (INTASC), which specifically outline what new teachers need to know and to be able to demonstrate. To help new teachers to continue to build on prior knowledge and skill, we think these standards should be used to guide the development of beginners for the first three years of their teaching career.

We view standards as tools for educators to use to guide their professional journeys. For the first time, the profession is beginning to clearly articulate what effective teaching and learning is all about. Standards, in our opinion, should not be used as sticks to beat teachers into submission or threaten their job performance; rather we think standards should be used as targets for individuals, schools, and systems to set clear and consistent goals. All teachers must be continually involved in the processes of goal-setting, self-monitoring, self-evaluation, and action planning to improve their performance. The more capable teachers judge themselves to be, the more challenging the goals they take on. New teachers in particular need to be engaged in individual and collaborative inquiry because it builds self-actualization and increases teacher efficacy.

Figure 7.1 presents an abridged version of the INTASC Standards. We have put them in a format to help the new teacher self-assess performance in the areas judged by the profession as key competencies for professional development of the beginning teacher. These standards provide both the new teacher and their mentors a common vocabulary upon which to reflect and analyze teaching behaviors and overall classroom performances. Here's what a newly trained teacher mentor had to say about standards:

Wanda's Journal

As I rated myself on the INTASC Standards for beginning teachers, I realized that in Standard Three: Diverse Learners, I do not use current knowledge of different cultural contexts within my community as I should....Since I am transferring to a new high school where twenty percent of our students will be Hispanic, I realize I will have to do a better job....Overall, I feel that I demonstrate these standards and model them well for my mentee....I have learned that collecting data based on standards puts me in the role of helper and not evaluator....My mentee was quite impressed that her teaching was being compared to these current teaching standards and best practices and not to my opinion.

In addition, we believe new teachers should identify areas that they find especially interesting and willing to pursue because they want to develop their expertise or knowledge base. In our opinion, this aspect of professional development has not been clearly emphasized. The objective here is to begin conversations about special interest topics that the new teacher is willing to investigate and perhaps become a peer resource/expert within the learning community. Two of the development needs of young adults are *the desire for active mastery of the environment and the natural inclination for excitement and idealism*. If we are to keep new teachers in the profession, it seems necessary to foster these areas of inquiry and support the new teachers' efforts in building expertise within them.

In collaboration with mentors and instructional supervisors, we suggest that the new teacher target specific standards for each of the first three years to really focus his or her competence building. This doesn't mean the teacher disregards any standards but rather outlines a strategic approach to ensuring that knowledge and skill is developed systematically and comprehensively. All ten of the INTASC standards and their corresponding indicators (knowledge, skills, and disposition) can be overwhelming. For professional development purposes, breaking them down into manageable components based on individual and school-level assessment needs seems a good way to reduce work overload.

Career Map 7.1. Individual Performance Assessment

Figure 7.1. INTASC Performance Standards

Standard 1: Content Pedagogy				
Understands the central concepts, tools of inquiry, and structures of the discipline and can create learning experiences that make these aspects of subject matter meaningful for students.				
	My Performance Expectations			
Performance Indicators	*Below*	*Meets*	*Exceeds*	*Research Interest*
1.1 Demonstrates knowledge of the central concepts of the discipline				
1.2 Uses explanations and representations that link curriculum to prior learning				
1.3 Evaluates resources and curriculum materials for appropriateness to the curriculum and instructional delivery				
1.4 Engages students in interpreting ideas from a variety of perspectives				
1.5 Uses interdisciplinary approaches to teaching and learning				

Standard 2: Student Development				
Understands how students learn and develop, and can provide learning opportunities that support students' intellectual, social, and personal development.				
	My Performance Expectations			
Performance Indicators	*Below*	*Meets*	*Exceeds*	*Research Interest*
2.1 Evaluates student performance to design instruction appropriate for social, cognitive, and emotional development				
2.2 Creates relevance for student by linking with their prior experiences				

Standard 3: Diverse Learners

Understands how students differ in their approaches to learning and creates instructional opportunities that are adapted to diverse learners.

	Performance Indicators	My Performance Expectations			
		Below	Meets	Exceeds	Research Interest
3.1	Designs instruction appropriate to students' stages of development, learning styles, strengths, and needs				
3.2	Selects approaches that provide opportunities for different performance modes				
3.3	Accesses appropriate services or resources to meet exceptional learning needs when needed				
3.4	Adjusts instruction to accommodate the learning differences or needs of students (e.g., time and circumstances of work, tasks assigned, communication, and response modes)				
3.5	Uses knowledge of different cultural contexts witin the community (e.g., socioeconomic, ethnic, cultural) and connects with the learner through types of interaction and assignments				

Standard 4: Multiple Instructional Strategies

Understands and uses a variety of instructional strategies to encourage student development of critical thinking, problem solving, and performance skills.

	Performance Indicators	My Performance Expectations			
		Below	Meets	Exceeds	Research Interest
4.1	Selects and uses multiple teaching and learning strategies (i.e., a variety of presentations/explanations) to encourage students in critical thinking and problem solving				
4.2	Encourages students to assume responsibility for identifying and using learning resources				
4.3	Assumes different roles in the instructional process (i.e., instructor, facilitator, coach, audience) to accommodate content, purpose, and learner needs.				

Standard 5: Motivation and Management

Uses an understanding of individual and group motivation and behavior to create a learning environment that encourages positive social interaction, active engagement in learning and self-motivation.

	Performance Indicators	My Performance Expectations			
		Below	Meets	Exceeds	Research Interest
5.1	Develops clear procedures and expectations that ensure students assume responsibility for themselves and others, works collaboratively and independently, and engages in purposeful learning activities				
5.2	Engages students by relating lessons to students' personal interests, allowing students to have choices in their learning, and leading students to ask questions and solve problems that are meaningful to them				
5.3	Organizes, allocates, and manages time, space and activities in a way that is conducive to learning				
5.4	Organizes, prepares students for, and monitors independent and group work that enables full and varied participation of all individuals				
5.5	Analyzes classroom environment and interactions and makes adjustments to enhance social relationships, student motivation/engagement and productive work				

Standard 6: Communication and Technology

Uses knowledge of effective verbal, nonverbal, and media communication techniques to foster active inquiry, collaboration, and supportive interaction in the classroom.

	Performance Indicators	My Performance Expectations			
		Below	Meets	Exceeds	Research Interest
6.1	Models effective communication strategies in conveying ideas and information and when asking questions (i.e., monitoring the effects of messages; restating ideas and drawing connections using visual, aural, and kinesthetic cues; being sensitive to nonverbal cues, both given and received)				
6.2	Provides support for learner expression in speaking, writing, and other media				
6.3	Demonstrates that communication is sensitive to gender and cultural differences				
6.4	Uses a variety of media communication tools to enrich learning opportunities				

Standard 7: Planning

Plans instruction based upon knowledge of subject matter, students, the community, and curriculum goals.

	Performance Indicators	My Performance Expectations			
		Below	Meets	Exceeds	Research Interest
7.1	Plans lessons and activities to address variation in learning styles and performance modes, multiple development levels of diverse learners, and problem solving and exploration				
7.2	Develops plans that are suitable for curriculum goals and are based on effective instruction				
7.3	Adjusts plans to respond to unanticipated sources of input and/or student needs				
7.4	Develops short- and long-range plans				

Standard 8: Assessment

Understands and uses formal and informal assessment strategies to evaluate and ensure the continuous intellectual, social, and physical development of the learner.

		My Performance Expectations			
	Performance Indicators	Below	Meets	Exceeds	Research Interest
8.1	Selects, constructs, and uses assessment strategies appropriate to the learning outcomes				
8.2	Uses a variety of informal and formal strategies to inform choices about student progress and to adjust instruction				
8.3	Uses assessment strategies to involve learners in self-assessment activities to help them become aware of their strengths and needs, and to encourage them to set personal goals				
8.4	Evaluates the effects of class activities on individuals and on groups through observation of classroom interaction, questioning, and analysis of student work				
8.5	Maintains useful records of student work and performance, and can communicate student progress knowledgeably and responsibly				
8.6	Solicits information from parents, other colleagues, and students about students' experiences, learning behavior, needs and progress				

Standard 9: Reflective Practice and Professional Development

Continually evaluates the effects of decision making—choices and actions—on others, and actively seeks out opportunities to grow professionally.

	Performance Indicators	My Performance Expectations			
		Below	Meets	Exceeds	Research Interest
9.1	Uses classroom observations, information about students, and research as sources for evaluating the outcomes of teaching and learning and as basis for experimenting with, reflecting on, and revising practice				
9.2	Uses professional literature, colleagues, and other resources to support self-development as a learner and as a teacher				
9.3	Consults with professional colleagues within the school and other professional arenas as support for reflection, problem solving, and new ideas, actively sharing experiences and seeking and giving feedback				

Standard 10: School and Community Involvement

Fosters relationships with school colleagues, parents, and agencies in the larger community to support students' learning and well-being.

	Performance Indicators	My Performance Expectations			
		Below	Meets	Exceeds	Research Interest
10.1	Participates in collegial activities designed to make the entire school a productive learning environment				
10.2	Links with counselors, teachers of other classes and activities within the school, professionals in community agencies, and others in the community to support students' learning and well-being				
10.3	Seeks to establish cooperative partnerships with parents/guardians to support student learning				
10.4	Advocates for students				

Step 2: Build Knowledge and Skill Based on Both Individual and Organizational Improvement Goals

For too long, teachers have been left out of the professional development loop. Many well-intended teacher development programs have focused primarily on the needs of the school system. We think that although this is important for improving the performance of schools and systems, the needs of the teacher to become an expert in some particular facet of teaching must also be nourished.

Teacher education programs need to do a better job of emphasizing that learning about being a teacher doesn't stop with the college degree. With new educational reforms taking place and the implementation of a standards-based teaching environment, every teacher needs to make a commitment to keep up-to-date about research and technology in their area of certification (Santrock, 2001).

For the new teacher, we think this encouragement will keep the teacher enthusiastic and optimistic about teaching by expecting her or him to not only meet the evaluation needs of the organization but also increase knowledge and skill in an area that they find intellectually challenging or intriguing. For lifelong learning to be ongoing, the adult learner must be able to set goals in areas that internally excite and motivate them to search for more data or set higher performance expectations. To accomplish this, the new teacher designs an action plan that shows both linkages to school improvement and individual improvement goals.

Figure 7.2 provides a format for customizing a professional development plan that we have experimented with. What do you like about this approach? What would you do differently?

Career Map 7.2. Designing a Customized Professional Development Action Plan

Figure 7.2. Customized Professional Development Action Plan

Part One: Self Assessment

Based on current experiences and knowledge base, I feel the following indicators are particular strengths:

INTASC Indicators of Strengths:

- Knowledge—What do you know as it relates to the indicator?

- Skills/Experiences—What can you do? What have you done in this area?

- Dispositions—What do you think is important?

Based on current experiences and knowledge base, I feel the following indicators are growth areas:

INTASC Indicators of Growth:

- Knowledge—What new information is needed?

- Skills/Experiences—What skills need to be learned or practiced? What experiences would be useful?

- What learning objective(s) do you target for this area?

Part Two: Collaboration with Mentor

- For each area of growth you should identify 1 to 3 objectives. List them in the table and then brainstorm activities that would best meet the objectives you have developed.

- Ask your mentor/supervisor to review your needs assessment, objectives, and activities.

- Revise after feedback

INTASC Indicators	Objective(s)	Activity

Part Three: Timeline and Evaluation

♦ After feedback finalize your objectives and activities.

♦ Now complete the action plan for implementation of the activities and assessment of the objectives.

INTASC Indicators	Objective(s)	Activity	Person Responsible	Timeline	Evaluate Results

Part Four: Approval for Plan

I have reviewed the INTASC Action Plan and approve of the activities as written by _____

Site Mentor: _____ Date:_____

Site Principal: _____ Date:_____

Step 3: Create Peer Development Learning Teams

Professional development does not occur in isolation. New teachers need to be assigned to Peer Development Learning Teams specifically for the purpose of sharing their individual professional development plans, communicating what they have learned through research and reflective practice, and documenting through assessment the impact of their activities on both their teaching performance and student learning. These teams should meet on a defined schedule and give new teachers from one to three year of experience opportunities to validate their learning experiences and to work together as learners. The team also provides a safe support group for beginning teachers and continues to change the teaching culture from one of professional isolation to one of professional collaboration. If we are serious about building authentic learning communities, then time and support for collegial interaction must start early in the career. These activities must be built into the master schedule on planned teacher workdays.

Margaret's Journal

As a new teacher, I was assigned to a Teacher Collegial Group. In my school, teachers are required to meet regularly to discuss specific instructional issues with each other. The principal selects a different focus topic each year. During my first year, we focused on effective teaching strategies for block scheduling. My peers presented on such strategies as cooperative learning, teaching to multiple intelligences, stress and time management, using reality therapy for discipline, effective ways to use direct instruction, and the integration of technology in the classroom. I found all these sessions to be very useful and really enjoyed the teaching demonstrations by my peers.

What can school systems do to change the organizational structure of the teacher workday to include time for professional learning and inquiry?

How can we build this necessary time into the calendar without requiring teachers to stay after school hours?

How can we convince parents that teachers need designated time without students to improve their practice and thus increase student achievement?

Step 4: Build Leadership Capacity

In this career framework, teacher leadership is viewed as a collective responsibility of all teachers. All teachers need to be involved in the process of improving schools. New teachers need to be encouraged to share their ideas and assume active roles in curriculum development and team leadership activities. However, we think this aspect should be limited to the indicators related to

INTASC Standard #10 (see Figure 7.1) during the first year and gradually expanded depending on the age, experiences, and development of the beginning teacher.

Step 5: Focus on Reflection and Quality of Impact on Teaching and Learning

In today's schools, effectiveness is measured in terms of gains in student achievement and improvement. Schmoker (1996) informs us that data is "an invaluable tool, capable of telling us how we are doing, what is and is not working, and how to adjust effort toward improvement" (p. 31). Likewise, data that documents teacher growth is also very important. The action planning process requires the new teacher to continually monitor and document increases in both knowledge and skills as they relate to student learning and achievement outlined by the INTASC Standards.

Many school systems are moving to professional portfolios in which teachers document growth over time on specified standards and also include evidence of high quality professional development activities, reflective practice, and linkages to the school's improvement plans. Figure 7.3 provides an approach that may assist in documenting the journey and contribute to such portfolios.

Career Map 7.3. Reflection and Evidence of Impact

Figure 7.3. Documenting That You Have Met INTASC Standards

Written Commentary
INTASC Standards

Overview

Teaching is a moral activity that implies thoughts about ends, means, and their consequences Moral activity is explicitly expressed in a school's curriculum. To be an effective school is of little matter unless the personnel within the organization first have defined what is meant by a good school—what should students learn and how they should learn it? (Glickman et al., 2001, p. 391)

Nature of This Assessment

In this written commentary, you will show how you have acquired important information and skills as they relate to teaching and learning. Through a written commentary and supporting artifacts, you will demonstrate how you have increased both knowledge and skills as targeted by the INTASC Standards.

What Do You Need to Do?

Submit a *Written Commentary and Artifacts* that describe and illustrate your approach in increasing knowledge and skill in your teaching performance and working collaboratively with peers to increase student achievement. Your commentary should be 3 to 5 pages in length. For this assessment, you need to show how you have met the indicators on the INTASC Standards you have targeted for professional growth.

Written Commentary

- *Your written commentary must address each standard targeted for professional growth as outlined in your action plan.* Identify each standard clearly by using headings and subheadings. You may address other standards.

- For each standard, demonstrate both your knowledge and skill, and show how this impacted your teaching and student learning.

- Support with references to the professional literature and data you have collected that address the indicators within the standard.

- Include in your description your assessment of knowledge and skill in this standard and possible recommendations to increase performance. References to feedback from your site mentor and any evaluations from your supervisor would strengthen your description.

INTASC Artifacts

For each standard targeted for growth, attach an artifact(s) that supports your commentary. Include a brief description that addresses these questions:

- Why did you select this artifact?

- What does this sample reveal about your knowledge and/or skill?

- What does this artifact reveal about impact on student learning?

How Should My Response Be Assessed

- The response contains clear and consistent evidence of the teacher's understanding of the standards and corresponding indicators.

- The response contains clear and consistent evidence of the teacher's ability to implement the standards and corresponding indicators with more than adequate knowledge and skill.

- The response provides clear and consistent evidence of the teacher's impact on teaching and learning in the classroom.

♦ The response is clearly written, without technical errors, and reflects the use of technology

Written commentaries such as these help the beginner to clarify what he or she has accomplished at the end of each semester or year. We think mentors and supervisors could read and comment on these summaries and use these reflections for dynamic conversations in tandem with end-of-year evaluations. Building-level mentors and instructional lead teachers might analyze the commentaries for recurring trends and use the data to structure local staff development for beginning teachers.

Step 6: Benchmarks for Teacher Inductees

What should we use to help the new teacher gauge progress? The literature on professional development tells us that it is difficult to both learn new skills and put them directly into practice with high levels of success. Guskey (2001) suggests that "fitting new practices and techniques to unique on-the-job conditions is an uneven process that requires time and extra effort, especially when beginning. Guidance, direction, and support with pressure are crucial when these adaptations are being made" (p. 6).

Here is a suggested outline of the signposts we could use to help the novices develop a well-rounded picture of their professional achievement.

Figure 7.4. Benchmarks for Beginning Teachers

Benchmarks	Year One	Year Two	Year Three
Summative Teacher Evaluation	80% of the evaluation criteria is rated Satisfactory or Better	80% of the evaluation criteria is rated Satisfactory or Better Some or all Satisfactory areas move to higher rating Any growth area(s) targeted move from Needs Improvement to Satisfactory	90% of the evaluation criteria is rated Satisfactory or Better No areas rated below Satisfactory Professional Licensure

Formative Self assessment INTASC	Development of action plan and written commentaries to guide professional learning based on INTASC Standardsd • Feedback from mentor and supervisor	Development of action plan and written commentaries to guide professional learning based on INTASC Standards • Feedback from mentor and supervisor	Development of action plan and written commentaries to guide professional learning based on INTASC Standards • Feedback from mentor and supervisor
Collaboration and Professional Inquiry	Beginning Teacher Support Group to address first-year concerns, identify potential problems, and collaborate with peers to find alternatives and solutions	Teacher Quality Inquiry Groups to focus on teaching demonstrations in front of peers in which expert thinking is valued and developed	Teacher Quality Inquiry Groups to focus on teaching demonstrations in front of peers in which expert thinking is valued and developed.
Staff Development Training Programs	Participation in both system-level and school-level staff development activities to meet targeted goals.	Begin Master's Program	Complete Master's Program T-5 Certificate
Special Interest Inquiry	Identification of key questions about practice and the plan to develop expanded expertise in an area of interest through research and classroom data	Action Research Activities on Special Interest Topic Peer Sharing of Information Learned	Action Research Activities on Special Interest Topic Peer Sharing of Information Learned

Step 7: Incentives and Rewards

We discussed earlier that teachers are motivated more by intrinsic rewards such as self-respect, responsibility, and a sense of accomplishment. Teachers measure their job success by such factors as involvement in decision making, using their skills in ways that are valued, having freedom and independence, being challenged, expressing their creativity, and having opportunities to learn. The question now becomes how we recognize and reward a competent performance. School communities will need to develop both intrinsic and extrinsic ways to promote and reward excellence.

Each school system is unique and has varying degrees of resources. Using the Career Map 7.4, brainstorm ways to reinforce the new teacher's achievement of increased knowledge and skills.

Career Map 7.4. Promoting and Recognizing Teaching Excellence

Figure 7.5. Intrinsic and Extrinsic Incentives and Rewards

	Intrinsic Incentives and Rewards	*Extrinsic Incentives and Rewards*
System Level		
School Level		
Team Level		

Career Stage Summary—Teacher Inductee

We have spent several chapters outlining what current best practice and research has to say about teacher induction and mentoring. So the next big questions are: "How does a school system make any of this happen? How do principals give beginners a lighter workload or fewer assignments? What can be done and what are the alternatives?" Here's what several school leaders have to say:

From the North Carolina State Board of Education...

The State Board of Education has adopted guidelines for optimum working conditions for beginning teachers. A beginning teacher should:

- ♦ Be assigned in the area of licensure
- ♦ Have a limited number of preparations
- ♦ Be given only a limited number of exceptional or difficult students

- Be provided an orientation including district and school expectations

- Have minimal noninstructional duties

- Have no extracurricular activities unless the beginning teacher requests them in writing

From the Principal's Desk...

I have been an elementary school principal for several years. In my large urban school district, several key components are in place for a quality induction and mentoring program. New teachers are given a week-long orientation program prior to preplanning week. Three of those days, new teachers spend in their schools where they meet with administrators/induction team as well as their assigned mentor and grade-level/department chair. During those three days, the beginners receive information about their school to include where and how to locate resources, profiles of their students, assigned classroom, faculty handbook, school spirit wear, tour of school, curriculum guides, etc. Their assigned mentor helps them along this journey. The beginner's grade-level/department chair arranges lunch with beginner and their assigned grade level/department colleagues. Two remaining days of the week-long orientation are conducted at the district level and are devoted to district-wide topics such as available resources, employee benefits, curriculum, etc.

Our school district also provides extensive mentor training for teachers recommended by a school selection committee. The mentor training includes 50 hours of coursework and 50 hours of internship and seminars all related to mentoring. Mentors receive stipends for completing the course as well as for mentoring a beginning teacher. Stipends are provided by the school district and the state DOE.

Although a major factor in the availability of the above experiences is dependent on financial support by the district (mainly stipends paid to beginners to report to work one week early, and to mentors), I have become more and more aware of how much power a principal has to provide a meaningful transition for our novice teachers. Many of those opportunities require minimal financial support and are within our scope of responsibility to provide. I will focus my comments on those areas.

Guidelines I use regarding beginning teacher induction and mentoring:

- *Limit the number of beginning teachers that I hire based on how many beginners the school can adequately support. There are currently 10 trained mentors in my school out of 55 teachers on faculty; however, I have found over time that 3 or 4 is* the maximum number of beginners that our school can support at a satisfactory level during a given year.

· Begin the interview/hiring process as early as possible so the beginner has every opportunity to be ready for the first day of school.

· Limit the number of special needs students assigned to the novice.

· Limit the number of students with challenging parents assigned to novice.

· Limit the number of preparations/academic levels assigned to novice.

· Assign an assistant/paraprofessional to help novice during preplanning week with room set up, preparation of materials, clerical duties, etc.

· Assign a trained mentor in the same subject area as novice. If one is not available, assign an in-school mentor and a mentor from another school who is teaching the same subject as the beginner.

· Provide release time for mentor and novice to observe each other, other teachers, attend conferences, and reflect on practices.

· Limit the number of extracurricular responsibilities, e.g., bus duty, school committees, meetings, etc., for beginner and mentor.

· Assign only one beginning teacher to a mentor.

· Conduct all observations (three) required by school district teacher evaluation instrument myself, rather than assigning some or all observations to assistant principal. A bond is formed between principal and novice.

· Provide additional funding for start-up needs of beginner. I usually allocate about $200 above what other teachers are allocated.

· Make first year evaluation as formative as possible. Specific feedback is more valuable and encouraging to beginners than a summative evaluation rating. I also offer to conduct informal observations for feedback only to beginners that would like that information.

· Establish role of induction team members. Members are: assigned mentor, grade level/department chair, curriculum support teacher, and administrator.

· Meet with mentor and beginner to establish expectations I have, as well as support I will provide.

· Provide materials and support for mentors. I provide each mentor with a copy of Coaching & Mentoring (2000), Podsen and Denmark, and The First Days of School (1998), Wong and Wong. In addition, I send mentors to professional conferences that would benefit them as mentors and life long learners.

Things I would like to do in the future:

· Form Beginning Teacher Support Group to address the unique needs of our novices. Group would meet once a month and I would attend also.

- Provide a Beginning Teacher Handbook.
- Provide end-of-first-year celebration for beginners and their mentors.
- Provide full-time assistant/paraprofessional help for beginners not only during preplanning but also during the first week of school. Although this assignment would result in less assistant/paraprofessional help for the other teachers during preplanning and first week of school, veterans would accept this as part of the school-wide commitment to help the beginner succeed.
- Ensure that beginning teachers hired after the beginning of school receive same quantity and quality support as those who were hired at the beginning of the school year.
- Provide strong support and professional development opportunities during the beginner's 2nd and 3rd years of teaching. They are ready to "kick it up a notch" and I need to help them do just that.
- Evaluate the induction/mentor program annually. Receive feedback from beginning teachers, mentors, grade-level/department chairs, and induction team.

References

Carr, J. F., & Harris, D. (2001). *Succeeding with standards: Linking curriculum, assessment, and action planning*. Alexandria, VA: Association for Supervision and Curriculum Development.

Glickman, C.D., Gordon, S., & Ross-Gordon, J. M. (2001). *SuperVision and instructional leadership: A developmental approach*. Needham Heights, MA: Allyn and Bacon.

Guskey, T. R. (1995). *Results-oriented professional development: In search of an optimal mix of effective practices*. http://www.ncrel.org/sdrs/areas/rpl_esys/pdlitrev.htm. Retrieved 2/15/01.

U.S. Department of Education. (1998). Promising Practices: The induction of new Teachers. Availalbe from: http://www.ed.gov/pubs/PromPractice/chapter5.htm.

Santrock, J. (2001). *Educational psychology*. New York: McGraw-Hill Higher Education.

Schomoker, M. (1999). *Results: The key to continuous school improvement*. Alexandria VA: Association for Supervision and Curriculum Development.

Sparks, G. M., & Loucks-Horsley, S. (1989). Five models of staff development for teachers. *Journal of Staff Development, 10*(4), 40–57.

Career
Stage Two:
Teacher Specialist

8

Fostering and Valuing Expertise

If teachers are to help transform their schools into professional learning communities, they must recognize their obligation to practice and explore the art and science of teaching for their entire careers. Furthermore, they must practice their profession in ways that will distinguish them from more conventional colleagues....

National Educational Service, 1999

The research suggests that ongoing professional development is essential if teachers are to increase their impact on student learning. In particular, early-level teachers need to expand their content knowledge and pedagogical skills within their subject area specialization. "It is a teacher's professional responsibility to examine, refine, and broaden his or her practice on a continuing basis" (McColsky & Egelson, 1993, p. 382). But, in order to do this, a culture of continuous cognitive reflection on curriculum and instruction must be valued and embedded in the professional learning community.

Profile of a Teacher Specialist

One of the adult development needs of teachers early in their teaching career is the desire for recognition, occupational advancement, and status. The Teacher Specialist Career Stage needs to center on helping every teacher remain enthusiastic and intellectually challenged. Let's review two journal excerpts by teachers who are involved in activities at their schools that seem to be meeting the needs of teachers in nontraditional ways.

149

Pat's Journal

During my early teaching years, I worked in a stagnant, but highly respected, school. Dialogue about curricular changes was unheard of. In fact, to encourage that dialogue, one would have probably been laughed at. I cannot imagine discussing with other teachers the curriculum we were using and the instructional changes needed to implement the curriculum. Instead for all those years, I shut my door and did my own thing. Now, years later, I am working in a much different setting. I am part of a group of educators that truly values education and is willing to take any risks to ensure students learn and are successful. We are involved members of the school community working on developing meaningful conversations about our practice so that ongoing professional dialogue becomes the rule and not the exception.

My principal really believes in cognitive coaching and regularly establishes planned peer coaching activities so we can assess our own thinking processes and practice making known to ourselves and our peers what do and why we do it. As a result of cognitive coaching sessions with my peers, I have explored the thinking behind my teaching behaviors. I discovered that I could not easily explain the reasons for my actions nor could I tie what I did to current teaching and learning theory and practices. This inability to quickly respond to the questions of my peers made me feel uneasy, and I began to question my motives and underlying assumptions for the teaching decisions made in a lesson. I also realized that I did not fully understand several of the learning models that I thought I was using and the scope of their impact on student learning. As a result of these coaching sessions I feel I can better self-analyze my teaching and express what I do by linking action to theory and best practices. This process has also helped me to be a better teacher mentor.

Chris' Journal

My principal is probably the best example of a teaching principal. She does whatever it takes to help us become a better learning community. For example, she believes that every teacher must become an expert within his or her teaching area and structures professional development plans to help us identify objectives that meet not only the school's mission and goals but, equally as important, our own professional goals and interests. Before working at this school, I was never asked what aspect of teaching I was passionate about and wanted to develop further expertise in. I had never really thought about my responsibility as a member of a learning community to contribute to the learning of my peers by sharing some aspect of my professional knowledge and skills.

I have always been a supporter of cooperative learning in the classroom. My professional interest is learning as much as I can about this approach and how I can use it to impact on student learning and their social skills development. I conducted my own action research on cooperative learning within my classroom and developed a system-level staff development workshop to help interested peers who also want to increase their skills in using this approach in their classrooms. I regularly model this instructional strategy for first-year teachers and team-teach with them when they begin to implement the approach in their classrooms. My principal has supported my goal by providing staff development funds for attendance at national training workshops and conferences dealing with this concept. She also gives me release time to work with beginning teachers interested in using cooperative learning.

**What is happening in these schools that is similar or different from what is
    happening in your school?**
What is the role of the principal in these schools?
How does the role of the principal impact on teacher development?

Continuing the Professional Dialogue

What happens to the new teacher after the first few years of teacher mentoring? Do you have a system in place to ensure the continued development of the novice—one that seeks to continue and build dynamic conversations about instructional practice and curriculum needs among teachers. What is your notion of a professional learning community?

Sergiovanni (1994) asserts that as principals and teachers inquire together, they create community. Inquiry forces debate among teachers about what is important and promotes a deeper understanding of decision making and the rationale for choices made in the instructional process. Reflective dialogue centers on staff conversations about teaching and learning and the impact of these processes on students. A review of a teacher's actions by colleagues is the key behavior in a professional learning community (Louis & Kruse, 1995). This is not an evaluative approach but more the interaction among critical friends.

So how do we create these professional communities? According to Hord (1997), "in studies comparing how teachers around the globe spend their time, it is clear that in countries such as Japan, teachers teach fewer classes and use a greater portion of their time to plan, confer with colleagues, work with students individually, visit other classrooms, and engage in other professional development activities" (Darling-Hammond, 1994, 1996). It becomes apparent that the role of the teacher needs to be studied and reviewed. *The idea that the only legitimate use of a teacher's time is standing in front of a class may be seriously outdated based on recent studies.* In particular, a summary report (Hord, 1997, p. 27) of results on staff outcomes in schools organized as professional learning communities indicates the following trends:

- Reduction of professional isolation

- Powerful learning that defines good teaching and classroom practice

- Creation of new knowledge and beliefs about teaching and learning

- Increased meaning and understanding of the content that teachers teach and the roles they play in helping all students achieve

- Higher likelihood that teachers will be well informed, professionally renewed, and inspired to inspire students

- More satisfaction, higher morale, and lower rates of absenteeism

- Commitment of making significant and lasting changes

- Higher likelihood of undertaking systemic change

The literature review on professional learning communities shows increasing data that teachers become more effective and student outcomes increase when a culture of reflective inquiry becomes a driving force in the workplace.

If we are really serious about building authentic learning communities, then time and support for collegial interaction must start early in the career and be sustained. Opportunities for teachers to dialogue about what they do must be planned and valued by the entire school community. The literature on professional learning communities clearly emphasizes the need for supportive conditions in the workplace (Boyd, 1992; Louis & Kruse, 1995). In Figure 8.1 we review several key factors outlined by both Boyd (1992) and Louis & Kruse (1995) that impact on the ability of teachers to come together as a learning community. Read each condition and assess how your school meets these factors:

Career Map 8.1: Assessing Your Professional Learning Community

Figure 8.1. Key Factors of Your School's Learning Community

Supportive Conditions in the Workplace	*1 Present and Consistent Highly Valued*	*2 Present but Not Consistent Moderately Valued*	*3 Not Present Not Valued*
Organizational Factors			
• Time to meet and talk			
• Schedules and structures that reduce isolation			
• Physical proximity of staff to one another			
• Interdependent teaching roles			
• Well-developed communication structure			
• School autonomy			
• Teacher empowerment; shared decision making			
• Staff input into selecting teachers and administrators			
• Availability of resources			
Human Factors			
• Willingness to give and accept feedback			
• Norms of critical inquiry and continuous school improvement			
• Respect and trust among colleagues			
• Ongoing individual/professional development			
• Supportive leadership from principal			
• Strong induction and mentoring processes			
• Positive teacher attitudes toward the profession			
• Focus on instructional improvement and students' heightened interest and engagement with learning			
• A sense of community			
• A sense that teachers can make a difference			

What does your assessment say about your working conditions for facilitating a professional learning community?

What are your strengths? Where do you need to go from here?

Looking at Adult and Teacher Development Needs

Earlier, in Figure 2.4, we outlined the adult development needs of teachers at specific point in their teacher development. Figure 8.2 presents a summary of these needs for the Teacher Specialist Career Stage.

Figure 8.2. Teacher Specialist: Adult Needs and Retention Risks

Career Stage	Adult Development Needs	Career Retention Risks
Teacher Specialist 23 to 35	• Era of greatest energy, abundance, contradiction and stress • Peak years biologically • A time for status and recognition and occupational advancement • Building an maintaining an initial adult life structure	• Job routine becomes boring • No advancements exist • Variety in the work nonexistent • Lack of flexibility in staffing patterns to accommodate family roles and professional development needs (i.e., job sharing, part-time work, sabbaticals) • Fragmented professional development that does not promote individual teacher input into goal setting, growth and expertise based on personal and professional goals • No incentives or rewards for seeking and attaining expertise

For the focus of this chapter, we think there are several key strategies that principals and school systems may need to consider in retaining teachers through their early years. Based on the risk factors identified for this career stage, the major threats seem to be: (a) job repetitiveness, (b) fragmented professional development that is not anchored in meeting both system level goals and individual professional interests, (c) no system of incentives or rewards to validate expertise, and (d) limited flexibility in job sharing opportunities and professional development options.

Job Boredom

Think about your experienced teachers. How would you describe them? Enthusiastic and growing, or stable and stagnant? Why do most of our veteran teachers seem to level off and stop pursuing intellectual challenges? We think the answer may lie in our indifference in providing the structure within staff development programs that focuses on developing their expert thinking skills.

According to Ethell & McMeniman (2000), the research documents that expert teachers are more knowledgeable than novices, but accessing the knowledge of the veteran teacher has not been clearly pursued. These researchers assert that the procedural knowledge of our experienced teachers is not articulated, and, for the most part, remains implied, and grounded in experience (Posner, 1967; Anderson 1982). Anderson (1990) explains that "the expert's increased experience facilitates the automation of procedural knowledge and the consequent freeing of the working memory to be utilized in higher-order cognitive skills necessary for the conceptual understanding of new knowledge" (Ethell & McMeniman, 2000, p .88). These researchers conclude that "many expert teachers lose their ability to articulate their knowledge as the automation of their procedural knowledge supersedes their declarative knowledge" (Beriter & Scaramalia, 1992; Berlinger, 1986; Resnick, 1989; Sternberg & Horvath, 1995).

So what does this mean? We believe that as teachers gain experience, the job of teaching gets *routinized* to the point of operating on autopilot. It means teachers perform complex tasks without really thinking about what they are doing, why they are doing it, and how it relates to the current knowledge base. The ability and the disposition to reflect upon teaching practice is recognized as a key factor in developing one's metacognition or thinking about specific teaching behaviors. However, how many of us have really given this process any serious thought and time? Failure to nurture the development of the cognitive thinking skills of our teachers, so they can clearly express the relationships between means and methods employed and results achieved, may contribute to job boredom and lack of motivation to increase competence.

What We Know about Cognitive Coaching

Cognitive coaching is based on the idea that metacognition—the process of being aware of one's own thinking processes—fosters insight into what we know and do. By providing opportunities for teachers to reflect on teaching behaviors and the rationale for decision making, they become more aware of their own thinking processes and better able to articulate what they do.

The process involves the modeling of self-appraisal and the self-management of cognition by the teacher. In modeling, the teacher expert explains thinking, instructional strategies, and decisions made by naming the teaching behavior and then explaining why this behavior was selected and the impact on student learning. The peer coaches stimulate reflection by asking key questions designed to prompt the teacher to think about certain aspects related to teaching and learning within the lesson demonstrated. The sole purpose is to help the teacher self-monitor, self-analyze, and self-evaluate the teaching performance (Garmston et al., 1993).

Figure 8.3 is a guided protocol you might try with your staff to help teachers make known the unspoken knowledge they have acquired and raise awareness levels of their ability to express this knowledge. We have used this process in the training of mentor teachers to help them realize that just having novices observe what they do may not be enough. Mentors must be able to communicate the complex thinking that underlies the observable behavior and help novices to compare their thinking with the thinking of the expert teacher.

Career Map 8.2. Expert Thinking— Making Known The Unknown

Figure 8.3. Protocol for Fostering Metacognition

Step One

- Prepare your teachers by reviewing the definition and purposes of cognitive coaching. Give out current articles and discuss the process.

- Ask them to come to the work session prepared to teach a typical lesson to a small group of their peers.

- Explain that the purpose of the activity is help them crystallize their thinking about the teaching behaviors they use and the reasons for their selection.

Step Two

- Review each phase of the training protocol and answer any questions.

- Divide teachers into small groups of five or six according to subject areas. Ask them to rotate through the roles of Expert Teacher, Facilitator, and Observer. Ask for volunteers in the first session.

- Limit the practice sessions to two or three teaching episodes in order to give ample time for inquiry and reflection.

Step Three

♦ At the conclusion of the work session, ask the teachers what new insights they have about teaching and learning that they did not have when the session began.

♦ Ask them how the cognitive coaching process challenged their thinking.

Demonstration Lesson of Expert Teacher

Phase One: Reflection on Planning and Intentions (5 minutes)

Before the teaching demonstration begins, the facilitator asks the Expert Teacher the following questions:

♦ *How did you go about planning this lesson?*

♦ *What criteria guided you in content development?*

♦ *What objectives did you target for this lesson? How did you arrive at these objectives?*

♦ *Where do they fall in the big picture of the curriculum sequence for these students?*

♦ *What principles of curriculum development form the basis for your planning processes?*

Phase Two: Reflection in Action (30 minutes)

The Expert Teacher begins the lesson and continues for about 10 minutes. The Peer Observers write down what the teachers says and does, taking anecdotal notes about the teaching behaviors demonstrated and the teacher's responses to question asked by the group Facilitator. Ten minutes into the lesson, the Facilitator directs the teacher to stop the lesson and asks the following questions:

Students

♦ *How would you describe the learning styles/abilities/interests of the students targeted for this lesson?*

♦ *Based on what you know about these students, how did you develop the lesson sequence?*

♦ *What personal learning theories or principles are evident?*

♦ *How do you believe students learn?*

The Expert Teacher continues the lesson for another 10 minutes. The Facilitator then stops the demonstration and asks these questions:

Lesson Delivery

♦ *What instructional strategies did you select for this lesson and for what reasons?*

♦ *What best practices and/or standards do you feel you modeled in this lesson?*

♦ *Overall, what learning theory drives your lesson development?*

♦ *Did you make any changes in the lesson when teaching it? What were the reasons for doing so?*

♦ *How did you plan to assess how the objectives of the lesson were being met?*

Classroom Management

♦ *How do you go about establishing and maintaining a positive learning climate in the class? What disruptions typically occur in this type of lesson? How do you deal with it?*

♦ *If no disruptions occur, what do you usually do to deal with disruptive behavior? How did you develop this approach?*

♦ *What classroom management principles form the foundation of your approach?*

The Facilitator asks the other observers if they have any questions about the lesson, any observable behavior they would like clarified, or further elaboration on any response to a question asked by the Facilitator.

Phase Three: Self-Evaluative Reflection (5-10 minutes)

At the end of the 20 minute lesson, the facilitator asks the Teacher to:

♦ Reflect on the lesson as a whole in light of the original objectives.

♦ Comment on the strengths and weaknesses of the lesson as it relates to system-level standards and/or competencies.

♦ Comment on any changes he/she would implement in teaching this lesson to future classes.

♦ Comment on the ability to express the relationships between means and methods employed and results achieved.

Phase Four: Peer Observer Reflection (5-10 minutes)

After the Expert Teacher has commented, the Facilitator asks the Observers to:

♦ Reflect on the lesson as a whole in light of the original objectives.

♦ Comment on the strengths and weaknesses of the lesson.

- ◆ Comment on any changes he/she would recommend in teaching this lesson to future classes.

- ◆ Comment on the ability of the Expert Teacher to make known the thinking processes involved in teaching this lesson and the linkages to current knowledge about teaching and learning theory and best practices.

One of the key goals of teacher mentoring is to help novices become autonomous and expert thinkers. But, in order to do this, we may need to step back and ensure that our veteran teachers are able to model this important process. Cognitive coaching provides the road map in helping mentor's to develop the mentee's mental processing. "The guiding principle of cognitive coaching is that instructional behaviors will not be affected until the inner thought processes of teachers are altered and rearranged "(Barnett, 1995). The mentor/coach serves as the mediator of another professional's cognitive development instead of a directive and critical evaluator of his/her teaching performance. The mentor must have skillful questioning skills, clarifying and probing the thinking of the teacher while remaining nonjudgmental.

Wanda's Journal:

Until this teacher mentor training course, the idea of cognitive coaching was new to me. I have learned that coaching is prompting and questioning, as well as guiding and supervising practice....I have been reminded how difficult change is—especially to adults. Getting others to change the way they teach is easier if the change comes from within. That is why cognitive coaching is so important. It fosters independence by providing personal insights into the learner's own thinking processes. It builds flexible, confident problem-solving skills, and encourages self-efficacy and pride. By using cognitive coaching with my mentee, she came to some of the same conclusions about her teaching that I would have suggested if I had to.

There is substantial research support that indicates that "when potential and practicing professionals are provided with systematic, well-designed programs aimed at developing their cognitive abilities, they measurably improve their reflective and problem-solving abilities....By implication, mentors who become cognitive coaches will require ongoing assistance in developing their own cognitive abilities and teaching skills" (Barnett, 1995, pp. 54–55).

Revamping Professional Development

For lifelong learning to be ongoing, adult learners must be able to set goals in areas that internally excite and motivate them to search for more data or set higher performance expectations. As the job of teaching becomes more constant, we must ensure that the developing teacher does not become apathetic about his or her career development. According to an AT&T personnel manager, for example, all executives are advised to spend approximately 10 percent of their job time on performance training and career expansion. Sparks and Loucks-Horsley (1989) suggest several ways, set forth in Figure 8.4, to keep teachers actively engaged in their own professional development:

Figure 8.4. Professional Development Options

Approach	Characteristics	Outcomes
Individually Guided Development	• Teacher self assesses and sets learning goals • Designs action plan • Implements action plan • Evaluates results	• Creates a sense of professionalism • Fosters individual empowerment • Enhances problem-solving skills
Peer Observation and Cognitive Coaching	• Teacher seeks feedback from colleagues on teaching practices through classroom observation • Observers collaboratively identify strengths and growth areas • Peer dialogue focuses on best practices • Both the observed teacher and peer observers learn in the process	• Builds team work • Reduces professional isolation • Sharpens observation, data-collection skills • Increases ability of teachers to connect current teaching behaviors to best practices, learning theories, and principles
Involvement in School Improvement Process	• Teacher becomes a member of a school improvement committee or task force • The team assesses current school situation, collects data, frames problems, generates possible solutions, and develops action plans to resolve problems identified	• Expands the role of the teacher beyond the classroom • Increases knowledge and skill in school improvement needs through developing curricula, designing programs, or changing practice based on school improvement goal • Builds teacher leadership skills and attitudes

Training Program	• Teacher participates in a particular program to expand knowledge and skill to meet either individual and/or school development needs • Effective programs include exploration of theory, demonstrations of practice, supervised trial of new skills with feedback, and coaching within the workplace	• Stimulates teacher thinking and notions of teaching and learning • Exposes teachers to external learning resources
Action Research Inquiry Teams	• Teachers formulate questions about their practice and develop action research plans to investigate possible answers • Individually or in teams, problems are identified, data is collected, analyzed, and proposed changes in classroom practice are recommended	• Fosters the idea of teacher as researcher • Enhances reflective action • Develops problem-solving and critical thinking skills • Cultivates professional learning community

To keep the experienced teacher intellectually vibrant, professional development plans need to consider all of these approaches as viable options for teachers to select as ways to challenge their thinking and rejuvenate their teaching practices. We next review, in Figure 8.5, a Performance Assessment Plan, what a large metro Atlanta, Georgia school system is doing to capitalize on several of these approaches. *We have highlighted those aspects that we think show a shift from traditional teacher evaluation and professional development models.*

> **What do you like about the approach this system has adopted? Compare to your system.**
> **What might you do differently and why?**

Career Map 8.3. Sample Performance Assessment Plan

Figure 8.5. Cobb County Performance Assessment Plan

Mission and Strategic Goals

The vision of our school system is to have a community with a passion for learning. These three strategic goals provide the framework for this vision:

1. Increase student achievement
2. Increase effective and efficient use of resources

3. Increase stakeholder satisfaction

Performance Assessment System for Classroom Teachers

In August of 1998, the Board created a Performance Improvement Committee on Staff Evaluation and Staff Development to research, develop, and implement an innovative assessment instrument for evaluating classroom teachers in the twenty-first century. The charge to the committee was to select or develop an evaluation instrument that focuses on student achievement and staff development.

In May of 2000, the Cobb County Board of Education adopted the committee's recommendation to implement the model for teaching based on Charlotte Danielson's book, *Enhancing Professional Practice: A Framework for Teaching* published in 1996.

The Performance Assessment System for Classroom Teachers satisfies both the need for accountability and the mutual desire of teacher and administrators for meaningful professional growth. This teacher assessment system is characterized by the following elements:

-   Both formative and summative assessment processes

-   *Self-directed professional growth for teachers*

-   *Clear criteria and standards that support the district's vision and goals*

-   Clear procedures for the evaluation of performance

-   *Ongoing training for both teachers and administrators*

These elements collectively provide the foundation for reliable, valid assessments for teacher performance. This instrument embodies five common themes:

-   Equity

-   Cultural diversity

-   High expectations

-   *Developmental appropriateness*

-   Integration of technology

The Cobb County School District *Performance Assessment System for the Classroom Teacher* reflects current trends:

-   The *use of multiple sources of information to evaluate teaching* in addition to direct classroom observation

-   *An emphasis on teacher self-assessment, reflection, and collegial support*

◆ *The use of multi-year assessment cycles with specialized procedures for teachers in different phases of the cycle*

The assessment system includes two different processes: a Formative Assessment process and a Summative Assessment process. These two processes are briefly summarized below and are described in more detail in Sections 3 and 4 of this manual.

Summative Assessment Process

The scope of the Summative Assessment process is broader than that of the Formative process. The Summative Assessment consists of an ongoing administrative review and formal assessment in each of the components in the Performance Assessment Instrument for Classroom Teachers. Approximately one-third of the classroom teachers will be evaluated in the Summative Assessment process each year.

This process includes classroom observations by an administrator, including pre- and post-observation conferences, meetings between the teacher and the administrator, *regular meetings for the teacher with a Focus Group*, and the comprehensive review of evidence of performance gathered by both the teacher and the administrator

Formative Assessment Process

Approximately two-thirds of the classroom teachers will be evaluated in the Formative Assessment process each year. Teachers completing the Formative Assessment process *conduct a self-assessment using the Performance Assessment Instrument, select (together with an administrator) suitable goals for focus, join a Focus Group to promote professional development, develop a professional growth plan, and implement that plan.*

The *teacher also sets student achievement goals and meets with the administrator* at the beginning of the school year *to obtain approval for goals.* The teacher and administrator meet at the end of the year to evaluate the progress toward attainment of these goals, and evaluate the teacher on Domain 4 of the Performance Assessment Instrument for Classroom Teachers.

Benchmarks and Standards

Establishing a professional learning community among teachers means creating opportunities for critical analysis and reflection on core issues about effective teaching practice. The National Board for Professional Teaching Standards (NBPTS) has designed a process that encourages experienced teachers to wrestle with questions like, "What is an accomplished teacher? What does an expert teacher do in the classroom? How does the professional teacher impact the lives of students and their learning?"

The National Board has centered their certification process on five central principles:

1. Teachers are committed to students and their learning

National Board Certified Teachers are dedicated to making knowledge accessible to all students. They act on the belief that all students can learn and they treat students equitably. They adjust their practice based on observation and knowledge of students.

2. Teachers know the subjects they teach and how to teach those subjects to students

National Board Certified Teachers have a rich understanding of the subjects they teach and appreciate how knowledge in their subject is created, organized, linked to other disciplines and applied to real-world settings….They command specialized knowledge of how to convey and reveal subject matter to students.

3. Teachers are responsible for managing and monitoring student learning

National Board Certified Teachers create, enrich, maintain, and alter instructional settings to capture and maintain the interest of their students. They are adept at setting social norms for social interaction among students and making the best use of instructional time. They can assess the progress of students individually and as a group.

4. Teachers think systematically about their practice and learn from experience

National Board Certified Teachers are models of educated persons, exemplifying the virtues they seek to inspire in their students….They engage in lifelong learning and strive to strengthen their teaching through critical reflection and adapting their teaching to new findings, ideas, and theories.

5. Teachers are members of learning communities

National Board Certified Teachers contribute to the effectiveness of the school by working collaboratively with other professionals on school improvement processes. They find ways to work with parents and engage them in the work of the school.

Here is an excerpt adapted from the NBPTS web page that captures the vision for expert teachers:

> According to NBPTS, *proficient teachers* search out other opportunities that will serve to *cultivate their own learning*. As savvy students of their own teaching, they know the value of asking others to observe and offer a critique of their teaching. They also know the value of writing

about their work and of soliciting reactions from parents and students. Thus, masterful teachers develop specialized ways to listen to their students, colleagues and administrators, and reflect on their teaching in order that they might improve their practice.

Able teachers are also *students of educational scholarship* and are cognizant of the settled and unsettled territory in their field. They stay abreast of current research and, when appropriate, incorporate new findings and appropriate technology into their practice. They take advantage of teacher centers and special conferences and workshops. They might conduct and publish their own research, if so inclined. The testing of new approaches and hypotheses is a commonplace habit among adept teachers, even if a normally overlooked and undocumented one.

Wise teachers *understand the legitimacy and limitations of the diverse sources that inform teaching* and they continuously draw upon them to enrich their teaching. Their enthusiasm for, and commitment to, continued professional development exemplifies a disposition they hope to nurture in students. Hence, the thinking, reasoning and learning that characterize first-rate teaching are doubly valuable: not only are thoughtful teachers able to teach more efficiently and effectively, they are also models for the critical, analytic thinking that they strive to develop in their students.

Teachers who are themselves *exemplars of careful reasoning*—considering purposes, marshaling evidence and balancing outcomes—are more likely to communicate to students the value and manner of such reasoning. Moreover, they model other dispositions and traits as well, such as a commitment to creativity in their work and the disposition to take risks in exploring new intellectual, emotional, physical or artistic territories.

Board certified teachers *know the subjects they teach and how to teach those subjects to students.* Teachers in command of their subject understand its substance—factual information as well as its central organizing concepts—and the ways in which new knowledge is created, including the forms of creative investigation that characterize the work of scholars and artists. Understanding the ways of knowing within a subject is crucial to the National Board Certified teacher's ability to teach students to think analytically. Critical thinking does not occur in the abstract, for the thinker is always reasoning about something.

Proficient teachers appreciate the fundamental role played by disciplinary thinking in developing rich, conceptual subject-matter understandings. They are dedicated to exposing their students to different modes of critical thinking and to teaching students to think analytically about content.

For the first time, the teaching profession has raised its voice and given us a vision of what a truly competent teacher should aspire to be. The bar has been set, and many of our colleagues have taken up the challenge to seek and achieve this benchmark. Teacher Specialists can use these standards or related national standards identified in their content-area specialization as guideposts in outlining their professional development goals.

To guide professional development plans, we suggest that teachers in the Specialist Career Stage use the NBPTS standards for their particular national certification area. All standards have been designed to help teachers focus their practice on student learning and are organized by categories. Figure 8.6 presents an overview of the standards for several certification areas. Complete standard descriptions for each certification area can be located on the NBPTS web page (http://www.nbpts.org) under "Candidate Resources."

Figure 8.6. NBPTS Standards Overview

Category	Early Childhood Generalist Ages 3 to 8	Middle Childhood Generalist Ages 7 to 12	Early Adolescence Through Adulthood Ages 11 to 18 Math	Exceptional Needs Ages Birth to 21
Preparing the Way for Productive Student Learning	Understanding Young Children Promoting Child Development and Learning	Knowledge of Students Knowledge of Content and Curriculum Learning Environment Respect for Diversity	Commitment to Equity and Access Knowledge of Students Knowledge of Mathematics Knowledge of Teaching Practice	Knowledge of Students Knowledge of Special Education Communication Diversity Knowledge of Subject Matter

Category	Early Childhood Generalist Ages 3 to 8	Middle Childhood Generalist Ages 7 to 12	Early Adolescence Through Adulthood Ages 11 to 18 Math	Exceptional Needs Ages Birth to 21
Advancing Student Learning in the Classroom	Knowledge of Integrated Curriculum Multiple Teaching Strategies for Meaningful Learning	Instructional Resources Meaningful Application of Knowledge Multiple Paths to Knowledge	The Art of Teaching Learning Environment Using Mathematics Technology and Instructional Resources Assessment	Meaningful Learning Multiple Paths to Knowledge Social Development
Supporting Student Learning through Long-Range Initiatives	Assessment	Assessment Family Involvement		Assessment Learning Environment Instructional Resources Family Partnerships
Professional Development and Outreach	Reflective Practice Family Partnerships Professional Partnerships	Reflection Contributions to the Profession	Reflection and Growth Families and Communities Professional Community	Reflective Practice Contributions to the Profession and to Education

Using these standards, teachers can continue to develop their expertise and concurrently prepare for national board certification, if they so choose to do so. Even if they do not, the process itself is a valuable professional development vehicle for all teachers. Here is what an Education Specialist student in North Georgia College & State University's (NGCSU) teacher leadership program said about her involvement in seeking and attaining national board certification:

Suzanne's Journal

In the fall of 1999, I achieved National Board Certification in the area of Early Adolescence Science. The National Board for Professional Teaching Standards aims to "establish high and rigorous standards for what accomplished teachers should know and be able to do. To gain certification, I have completed an in-depth self-evaluation of my teaching practices. This evaluation consisted of both an extensive portfolio and assessment. The portfolio required me to plan, implement, and reflect upon several lessons. It also examined my ability to assess student performance. Finally, it evaluated the extent to which I collaborated with other professionals to promote learning. The assessment exercise evaluated my content knowledge of physical, earth, and life sciences.

Becoming nationally certified has positively impacted my students as well as the colleagues with whom I teach. Because I am now a more reflective teacher, my lessons are more effective. The title of National Certified Teacher has enhanced the respect of my colleagues and as a result, they rely on me as a resource for improving student learning.

Career Map 8.3. Standards-Based, Customized Professional Development Plan

Through self-analysis and individualized professional development plans, early-level teachers can continue to analyze and improve their practice. Using the format introduced in the induction phase (see Figure 7.2), the advancing teacher now shifts the focus from the INTASC Standards for beginning teachers to those standards established by the National Board for Professional Teaching. These standards require higher levels of knowledge and skill and are more specific to the teacher's area of specialization. This continual reflective analysis process is the missing component in most professional development approaches for teachers. This component asks teachers to take on the responsibility of designing and monitoring their own career advancement.

Figure 8.7. Standards-Based, Customized
Professional Development Plan

Part One: Self-Analysis

Based on current experiences and knowledge base, I feel the following NBPTS indicators are emerging strengths:

NBPTS Standards of Strengths:

- ◆ Knowledge—What do you know as it relates to the target standard?

- ◆ Skills/Experiences—What can you do? What have you done that supports your assertions?

- ◆ Dispositions—What values and beliefs do you have about this area?

Based on current experiences and knowledge base, I feel the following NBPTS indicators are growth areas:

NBPTS Standards of Growth:

- ◆ Knowledge—What new information is needed?

- ◆ Skill—What skills need to be learned or practiced?

- ◆ What learning objective(s) do you target for this area?

Part Two: Approaches and Activities to Meet Objectives

- ◆ For each area of growth you should identify 1 to 3 objectives. List them in the table and then brainstorm activities that would best meet the objectives you have developed.

- ◆ Ask your peer coach to review your needs assessment, objectives and activities.

- ◆ Revise after feedback.

NBPTS Standard	Objective(s)	Activity
		• Individual Plan • Observation/Coaching Plan • Training Program • School Improvement Process • Action Research Plan

Part Three: Timeline and Evaluation

- ◆ After feedback, finalize your objectives and activities.

♦ Now complete the action plan for implementation of the activities and assessment of the objectives.

NBPTS Standard	Objective(s)	Activity	Person Responsible	Timeline	Evaluate Results

Part Four: Approval for Plan

I have reviewed the NBPTS Action Plan and approve of the activities as written by
_____

Peer Coach: _____ Date:_____
Site Principal: _____ Date:_____

Seeking and attaining NBPTS certification is not the only way we can measure teacher growth and professional accomplishments. Other benchmarks can include conducting and publishing action research, designing and implementing staff development workshops for peers and colleagues, presenting at national conferences, publishing articles and books, adding to one's certification area, and receiving honors and recognitions for one's professional knowledge and skills (i.e., Teacher of the Year). These are just a few examples of the ways teachers can benchmark and gain recognition for their expertise.

> **What other benchmarks would you add to this list?**
>
> **What incentives and rewards should be in place to recognize and value these contributions?**

Incentives and Rewards

The big question for the professional learning community is how to provide incentives and rewards for teachers with excellent track records. In most cases, the drive to succeed will be a personal one, and the reward will be accomplishing specific goals that are internally driven. However, if we are to sustain a corps of truly competent professionals, a baseline of clear incentives and rewards needs to be formalized. Here are a few possible ideas for you to think about:

- *Stipends* for particular benchmarks achieved. These are one-time distributions that recognize the level of achievement.

- *Staff development funds* to pursue approved goals and objectives as outlined in the action plans

- *Letters of recognition and special awards* banquets to publicize the achievements of teachers.

- Special *system-level publications* identifying teachers who have distinguished themselves and a brief description of their achievement.

- *Release time* for professional conferences and financial support to attend.

- *Reduction in workload* for teacher to share expertise, conduct action research, or develop staff development work sessions for peers.

- *Teacher on Special Project Assignment*—Teacher is released from all teaching assignments to learn, develop, lead, implement a project of importance for the school (i.e., develop a teacher mentoring program).

> What would you add to this list? What recommendations would you make to
>   your superintendent?
>
> What resources do you have to provide incentives and rewards? What do you
>   need?

Rethinking Staffing Patterns

Another risk factor for losing teachers from our schools in the Teacher Specialist Career Stage is the lack of flexibility in meeting the needs of family roles and childrearing demands. Many early-level teachers begin their families between the ages of 25 and 30 and do not want to work full time. What does your school system do to keep these young professionals involved in the school system until they are ready to return on a full-time basis?

What if job sharing is viewed as an important way to retain and keep current the job skills of teachers? What if teachers could work part-time in their schools to help with mentoring new teachers, completing special education paperwork, training substitute teachers, developing new programs, team-teaching with colleagues needing peer assistance, sharing a full–time teaching position, or working as a teacher leader on a special project? The list is endless, and the benefits to your staff and students are beyond measure.

> What limitations exist in your school or system to prevent teachers from work-
>   ing on a part-time basis?
>
> What can you do at your school to capitalize on the teaching expertise of teach-
>   ers needing personal/professional leave but who would consider working
>   part-time?

Janet's Journal

My mentee is an experienced teacher returning to education after being a full-time mom for 12 years. She is married with two children, ages 10 and 13. I would describe her as at the beginning of middle adulthood because she recently celebrated her 40th birthday. After much discussion, she and I both feel that she is making the midlife transition in that she feels that she is more compassionate, more reflective, and can see that everything is not "black or white." She laughed when she described herself as not feeling like a kid anymore.

In her teaching career, I would describe her as at the professional or teacher specialist level. My mentee has worked in the business community, has been involved in charitable organizations where she held various leadership positions, and has acquired her Master's degree. I think there is a side of my mentee that also demonstrates her emerging expertise. She is the only teacher in our department who teaches Business Law, and she has a passion for it. She is constantly reflecting and doing action research in this area. She has a real passion for teaching and loves her students.

My mentee has identified three areas that she needs assistance with in the area of Computer Applications: Planning for instruction, using a variety of teaching methods, and facilitating group discussion. We are working on action plans to meet these needs. She can't believe how things have changed since her first years as a business education teacher. When she left teaching to raise her family, she remembers teaching typing on typewriters and teaching accounting using only calculators. She commented that as her children got older, she would have considered part-time employment in the school system had it been available so she could have kept her teaching skills current.

Career Stage Summary: Teacher Specialist

How do we go about transforming the conventional school into a professional learning community? The task is not an easy one even under the best conditions. We have asked school principals to share what they do and what they might do differently in moving toward this goal.

From the Principal's Desk...

One of my major goals as a building principal, is to have a school filled with educational vitality: students actively learning, teachers actively learning, and administrators actively learning. Lifelong learning, alive and well! Several basic factors have promoted that environment of inquiry:

- Provide and secure time to meet and talk. During the school day, teachers at each grade level/department have a common planning time when they plan together, meet with curriculum support teacher and administrators, and engage in meaningful dialogue with each other. In addition, grade levels/departments meet after school on a regular basis. Faculty meetings usually are only once a month and always devoted to staff development experiences. The challenge for me as principal is to protect those times for growth and inquiry for teachers from the myriad of requests to use that time for school district issues, PTA requests, report requirements, and all the other "stuff" that consumes our precious time together. "Please tell your teachers to …," "I'd like to talk to the teachers about…" My job is to be the gatekeeper and diplomatically say "no."

- Physical proximity. Teachers tend to talk with teachers closest in proximity. To use that trend to prevent isolation and encourage dialogue, I assign classrooms by teachers' strengths and commonalities. First priority is to assign rooms to grade levels/departments in close proximity. If one teacher is strong in language arts and another in mathematics, I might assign them near one another to encourage dialogue and expanding expertise. New teachers are assigned classroom next to their mentor ideally; at least by a strong, collaborative teacher at that same grade level or subject area. No one is assigned a class in a portable without a good team-mate in an adjoining classroom portable.

- Continuous staff development opportunities. Many on-site staff development opportunities are offered for our teachers as well as an extensive array of professional development courses provided by the school district. Our most significant staff development has been on-site over time and all of our faculty participated. The power of common experiences and language is phenomenal. Teachers are offered the opportunity to attend many state and national conferences in an effort to stay abreast of new practices and programs. Those teachers seeking higher degrees are supported in their journey by reducing extracurricular demands to show lifelong learning is supported in our school.

- Self-initiated professional growth. Because we value self reflection and improvement, teachers take charge of their own professional growth annually through their Individual Growth Plan. Teachers develop goals, strategies, and assessment criteria to not only support the local School Improvement Plan but to also guide themselves in whatever professional growth they feel is best for them. It then becomes my job to make sure they have all the resources necessary to meet those goals. Progress on these goals is discussed at end of year and new goals for the following year begin to emerge.

- Encouragement to pursue grants. Our school district supports and awards mini-grants to teachers to support classroom innovations. Not only individual teachers but also entire grade levels/departments receive grants to pursue identified areas of growth that will impact student achievement. Every teacher in our building at one time or another has been the recipient of grant resources.

- Support for risk takers. I must be willing to take the heat when projects fail. Teachers need to feel secure to take risks and know that the rug will not be pulled out from under them even when they falter, as they are bound to do. I share in their "stumbles" and try to brush them off and frequently say, "Try it and good luck. Let me know how it goes." I share my successes and failures so they can see a model of risk taking by their administrator.

- Frequent recognition. Teachers are recognized for accomplishments, endeavors, and attempts through my monthly staff newsletter, personal notes from me (if only to say, "I heard something good about you today."), local newspapers, school district newsletter, superintendent and school board commendations. Every morning as students are arriving, I stop by every classroom and speak to the teacher using that "sweet moment" to pat them on the back.

- Open flow of communication. I attend grade-level meetings periodically without an agenda but rather to listen and encourage a culture for teachers asking, "Why? Why don't we...? What would happen if ...?" Then my job is to say, "What is getting in your way of doing what you feel you need to do?" I set about trying to reduce or remove those barriers while keeping teachers updated on what I'm doing and how it's going.

Things I would like to do:

- Guide teachers to develop their area of passion and expertise. Encourage them to develop their personal growth plan around areas of expertise. Helping them to soar! I like this approach better than always concentrating on weak areas.

- Recognize small successes along the way not just when the project is complete.

- Set up Cognitive Coaching teams to increase our ability to reflect on our own teaching.

- Increase my knowledge about National Board Certification and encourage faculty to pursue. Design ways to help expedite this process for them.

- Create more opportunities for dialogue across grade levels and departments.

References

Anderson, J. R. (1982). Acquisition of cognitive skills. *Psychological Review, 89*(4), 369–406.

Anderson, J. R. (1990). *Cognitive psychology and its implications* (3rd ed.). New York: Freeman.

Barnett, B. (1995). Developing reflection and expertise: Can mentors make the difference? *Journal of Educational Administration, 33*(5), 45–59.

Bereiter, C., & Scardamalia, M. (1992). Cognition and curriculum. In P. Jackson (Ed.), *Handbook of research on curriculum* (pp. 517–542). New York: Macmillan.

Berliner, D. C. (1986). In pursuit of the expert pedagogue. *Educational Researcher, 15*(7), 5–13.

Bohen, D. B. (2001). Strengthening teaching through national certification. *Educational Leadership, 58*(8), 50–53.

Boyd, V. (1992). *School context: Bridge or barrier to change.* Austin, TX: Southwest Educational Development Laboratory.

Darling-Hammond, L. (1994, November). *The current status of teaching and teacher development in the United States.* New York: Teachers College, Columbia University.

Darling-Hammond, L. (1996, March). The quiet revolution: Rethinking teacher development. *Educational Leadership, 53*(6), 4–10.

Fitts, P. M., & Posner, M. I. (1967). *Human performance.* Belmont, CA: Brooks/ Cole.

Hord, S. M. (1997). *Professional learning communities: Communities of continuous inquiry and improvement.* Austin, TX: Southwest Educational Development Laboratory.

Louis, K. S., & Kruse, S. D. (1995). *Professionalism and community: Perspectives on reforming urban schools.* Thousand Oaks, CA: Corwin Press.

McColskey, W., & Egelson, P. (1993). *Designing teacher evaluation systems that support professional growth.* Greensboro, NC: Southeastern Regional Vision for Education, School of Education, University of North Carolina at Greensboro. (ERIC Document Reproduction Service No. ED367662)

National Board for Professional Teaching Standards. Available from: http:// www.nbpts.org

Resnick, L. B. (Ed.). (1989). *Knowing, learning and instruction: Essays in honor of Robert Glaser.* Hillside, NJ: Erlbaum.

Schon, D. (1987*). Educating the reflective practitioner: Toward a new design for teachinf and learning in the profession.* San Francisco: Jossey-Bass.

Sergiovanni, T. J. (1994). *Building community in schools.* San Francisco: Jossey-Bass.

Sparks, G. M., & Loucks-Horsley, S. (1989). Five models of staff development for teachers. *Journal of Staff Development, 10*(4), 40–57.

Teacher Specialist: Resources and Internet Tools

http://www.ncrel.org
North Central Regional Educational Laboratory

Professional Development

www.ncrel.org/pd

Offers a step-by-step planner to help schools in designing and implementing professional development based on best practices of award winning schools.

Pathways to School Improvement

www.ncrel.org/pathways

A comprehensive assessment tool to help schools and teachers assess current performance in curriculum, instruction, and assessment. Also includes the content areas and students at risk as well as parent involvement, professional development, and educational technology.

http://www.funderstanding.com
Funderstanding: The Coolest Kids' Site

Provides concise research summaries and resources on current teaching and learning theories and applications in the classroom. Useful resource to help teachers in linking what they do to best practices as part of the cognitive coaching process.

Career
Stage Three:
Teacher Leader

9

Teachers Leading Teachers

Real leaders are ordinary people with extraordinary determina-
tion. It takes courage to push yourself to places that you
have never been before...to test your limits...
to break through barriers

NASSP, Great Quotations,
1985

Look carefully at your teaching faculty? What do you see? As the school leader, do you feel lonely at the top? How many of your teachers would you describe as *initiators* of important school changes and involved *supporters* of school improvement? What is your view of teacher leadership? These are important questions to consider if school improvement is your goal and you feel the majority of your teachers are not actively seeking ways to put their leadership skills to work.

Key Question—What Is Your Notion of Teacher Leadership?

Katzenmeyer and Moller (1996, 2000) tell us that many "school leaders are unaware of the potential of teacher leadership" and have very narrow views of what teacher leadership means (p. 2). For many building-level administrators, teacher leaders merely serve as facilitators of administrative directives to their departments or teams and act as communication buffers between teachers and administrators. Do your team leaders, department chairs, and curriculum coordinators serve as representatives rather than leaders who enact change (Livingston, 1992)? Where do you stand on this issue?

Look back on your Leadership Capacity Score on the Teacher Retention Perception Profile Inventory (see Figure 3.1). What are your strengths and growth areas?

181

Building leadership capacity means expecting all teachers to take the point position at some time in their professional career to move the school forward in accomplishing strategic planning goals and objectives. All teachers must face the realization that if they fail to embrace their responsibility to provide leadership needed in their schools, then we will continue to fall behind in our efforts to improve schools. As school leaders, we must seriously examine how teacher leadership is defined and the conditions that are needed to empower the leadership capacity within our schools (Carnegie, 1986; Holmes, 1986).

Defining the Teacher Leader

So, what is a teacher leader? If we look at Figure 9.2, our adult development chart and potential risk factors for this career stage, we might begin to define a teacher leader as (a) a maturing adult who desires higher status and responsibility within one's career and among the work group; and (b) an expert teacher who wants to share professional knowledge and skill in order to make a difference both within the classroom and beyond (McLaughlin, 1988). This means teacher leaders should have demonstrated competence in their teaching field and high professional credibility among their peers.

Katenmeyer and Moller (1996, 2000) contend that "teachers who are leaders lead within and beyond the classroom, influence others toward improved educational practice, and identify with and contribute to a community of teacher leaders" (p. 6). Pellicer and Anderson (1995) assert that "teachers have always been leaders regardless of whether or not their leadership has been fully acknowledged" (p. 7). They conclude that teaching inherently involves leading at the classroom level. A review of the literature on effective teaching indicates that accomplished teachers demonstrate key executive functions when they:

- Plan a course of action for teaching their content

- Communicate the learning objectives to their students

- Implement and orchestrate the learning activities

- Establish a businesslike climate for learning

- Motivate the learners and develop productive work groups

- Monitor the learners and guide their progress

- Assess performance of the learners and impact of their teaching

- Record and provide feedback to all stakeholders

Career Map 9.1.
What Is Teacher Leadership?

Figure 9.1. Teacher Leadership Criteria

Write down your ideas on the following points:

Define the term teacher leader.	
What percent of your faculty would you describe as active teacher leaders?	
List the tasks you assign to your teacher leaders.	
What barriers exist at your school that inhibit teacher leaders?	
What benefits do you derive from teacher leaders?	

Figure 9.2. Teacher Leader: Adult Needs and Retention Risks

Career Stage	Adult Development Needs	Career Retention Risks
Teacher Leader 30 to 45	• Termination of early adult-hood and the start of middle adult hood • Advancement to higher status and responsibility is important.	• No clear role expansion and expectation for all teachers to move into leadership roles both within and outside the classroom. • No strong sense of a learning community. • No strong sense that one can make a difference • Workload demands and lack of time • Personal and family role demands • Paralysis by accountability demands • Taboo among peers to accept or show leadership • Stagnation and mental disengagement

Wasley (1991) defined teacher leadership as "the ability to engage colleagues in experimentation and then examination of more powerful instructional practices in the service of more engaged student learning" (p. 170). Roland Barth (1999) described teacher leadership as the "act of having a positive influence on the school as well as within the classroom" and one Rhode Island teacher summarized the term as "…initiatives by teachers which improve schools and learning" (p. 11).

Without a clear definition of teacher leadership and the expectation that all teachers are leaders and will need to take an active part in the school improvement process, schools cannot move forward (Pellicer & Anderson, 1995). We can no longer continue to conduct business as usual and leave untapped a wealth of teaching and leadership expertise. Furthermore, failure to formally include the role of teacher leader in the professional career stage denies the internal needs of the adult to validate their life's work and expertise and become an influential agent in (a) helping those less experienced or less skilled in developing their teaching potential and (b) moving their schools forward (Troen & Boles, 1992).

In their book, *Awakening the Sleeping Giant*, Katenmeyer and Moller (1996, 2000) sum it up:

Within every school, there is a sleeping giant of teacher leadership that can be the catalyst to push school reform....By using the energy of teacher leaders as agents of school change, the reform of public education stands a better chance to succeed. School change is a complex, dynamic process and demands the best of everyone. We can no longer ignore the leadership capability of teachers, the largest group of school employees and those closest to the students. Empowered teachers bring an enormous resource for continuously improving schools. p. 2

What Do Teacher Leaders Do?

Leadership has many aspects and as many definitions. For our discussion, we will define leadership as the ability to move a group to accomplish a specific goal or action. Teacher leaders all have one common characteristic—they usually have the respect of their peers because they are exceptionally competent in their teaching area and have a very positive impact on student learning and classroom management.

Teacher leaders function in a wide range of roles and tasks. Pellicer and Anderson (1995) summarized these functions as (a) assuming responsibility for induction and mentoring of colleagues; (b) providing curriculum leadership in their content areas through work on curriculum committees, developing instructional materials, and conducting staff development workshops; and (c) serving in more formal roles as lead teachers, department chairs, grade chairs, coordinators, teachers on special assignment, and teacher mentors. (Lieberman et al., 1988; O' Conner & Boles, 1992)

Here are excerpts of teachers who were asked to describe both school level and professional community leadership experiences that they felt reflected their teacher leadership abilities. As you read the summaries, jot down the roles and tasks they experienced. Then compare these tasks with those you listed in Career Map 9.1.

Jane's Journal

Elementary School Teacher—4th Grade
Teaching Experience—11 Years

This past year (2001) I had the opportunity to be a participant in a technical training course for teachers and administrators. It was a significant experience for me because it afforded me the opportunity to work with my colleagues in a rich, challenging learning environment....I was able to work with one of our Kindergarten teachers to partner our students in the computer lab lessons using Graph Club and Print

Shop….Our increasing use of technology is ongoing. The computer isn't just for games anymore…..We have used this technology training to help our students research, write, create presentations, and develop brochures. Other teachers viewed these published products and wanted to know, "How did you do that? What program did you use? How long did it take? Will you show us how?" I am fortunate to have been on this early team from our school to increase my own technology competence as well as being able to share this knowledge and skill with students and other teachers. I have been asked to develop a workshop to help train our teachers in the use of technology in the classroom.

Last year I served as the Student Support Team (SST) Liaison for my grade level. The SST reviews students having difficulty in the school setting, whether academically, socially, emotionally, or physically. As the contact, my role was to have or find the necessary paperwork, document our meetings, arrange scheduling for all required participants, make suggestions for interventions, and log all meetings.

In the summer of 2000, I had the wonderful opportunity to work with Georgia Public Broadcasting's Peachstar Network to evaluate a social studies video library. A group of selected teachers met for a week to work on this project. It was stimulating to work with so many different people outside my own school….My role was to serve as the leader for my small team of reviewers….We were charged with recommending the grade levels that would benefit from the videos reviewed. This was a daunting task because we had to familiarize ourselves with curriculum different from our own, while remaining within the framework of the state's Quality Core Curriculum requirements…

Bob's Journal

Middle School Teacher—6th Grade
Teaching Experience—13 Years

Mentoring has been one experience that I have participated in at our school. I have mentored four teachers who were new to the school, three of which were first-year teachers. This experience has been significant to me because it helped me to learn to be more aware of and more organized with my duties as a teacher. Mentoring has also assisted me to think more deeply about my impact on other teachers as well as my students. This has helped me to be more conscious of the needs of others. The mentoring experience has made me more accepting of new ideas and strategies to try with students. Being a teacher mentor has increased my confidence level with my own teaching abilities and identified my personal strengths and growth areas as a mentor for future consideration.

I currently serve as the grade-level chairperson....My role includes: (a) conducting grade-level meetings with teachers to communicate information from the principal or other faculty members; (b) discussing concerns and issues related to the sixth grade; (c) gathering data from the grade-level teachers to give to the principal; (d) scheduling, organizing, and implementing activities for the grade level; (e) ordering materials for the grade level; and (f) representing the grade level on the School Leadership Committee.

I served as a member of the Math Advisory Committee for the County. This experience is significant because it allowed me to participate in a group that is involved in making decisions about math curriculum, textbooks, and ideas....My role included recommending a math series to be adopted by the Board of Education, and comparing and aligning the Georgia QCC's to national standards. This experience has had an impact on the professional community, because in the past, teacher input into this type of decision making was not valued. Now, teachers are being allowed to help make decisions and provide feedback on topics and issues that directly affect our work.

Susan's Journal

High School Teacher—Biology
Teaching Experience—15 Years

One significant experience within the last five years was that of Department Chair for the science department. As department chair, I was the instructional lead teacher for eight other colleagues. Each week, I reviewed lesson plans and impacted teaching and learning by making comments and suggestions for new activities and labs. I was trained as an evaluator in the Georgia Teacher Evaluation Program (GTEP). While serving in this role, I was able to offer constructive suggestions to teachers throughout the school as I completed my observations. As a department chair, I was a member of our school's leadership team, which meets monthly to discuss instructional issues as they arise. I was an advocate for our science teachers and our students in convincing my principal to divide a large classroom into two, creating a mini-computer lab for our science students. Having the lab right in the science department has allowed the students to use the Internet for research and to explore interactive science lab sites.

Another significant leadership role was that of Facilitator for a Teacher Collegial Group (TCG). As a group facilitator, I was responsible for scheduling meetings, notifying (reminding) members to come, and for introducing topics for discussion. The principal chooses a different focus topic each year. During school year 1999–2000, we focused on effective teaching strategies for block scheduling. I taught the members of my group in areas such as cooperative learning, teaching to multiple intelligences, stress and time management, using reality therapy for discipline, effective ways to use direct instruction, and the integration of technology in the classroom. The other teachers in my group depended on me to present the material and to lead the discussion about how each of us could use the strategy in our classrooms.

In June 2000, I was promoted to the position of Learner Support Strategist (LSS) for our high school. I have thoroughly enjoyed this role. As the LSS, I am considered a master teacher. As such, I am to use my classroom expertise to encourage my colleagues to deliver the best possible instruction to our students. I have been responsible for overseeing all our Teacher Collegial Groups this year. I have organized our staff development activities and monitored our level of achievement in each of the areas of our school improvement plan. I have helped to implement the administration of the Stanford Achievement Test to our students. I played an important role in our system's Teacher Induction Program. This was especially effective because I helped interview some of our new faculty members, so we established a good relationship from the beginning of the year. The new teachers felt comfortable coming to me for suggestions and help. I have written sample lesson plans, helped to develop rubrics for assessing students, and have even modeled some lessons in classrooms.

I am privileged to be a member of Alpha Delta Kappa honorary sorority for women educators. ADK is an international organization. Membership has afforded me the opportunity to meet many educators locally and across the state of Georgia. Since my induction in 1991 as a charter member of the County chapter, Gamma Delta, I have remained active in the sorority and held several different leadership positions. Examples are budget chairman, ways and mean chairman, corresponding secretary, and historian. I have held the offices of corresponding secretary, and historian.

I also served this year as co-chairman for a volunteer committee to investigate the possibility of adopting a modified calendar for school year 2001–2002. The committee was comprised of teachers from each of the seven schools in our county .I was responsible for scheduling meetings and for facilitating discussions that arose as we completed our research. Our committee was ultimately responsible for developing the proposed "modified" calendar that was put before our local board of education for consideration.

This experience introduced me to a lot of new faculty members from around the county. We were able to see how the calendar would potentially impact each school in a very different way. We learned about testing schedules, the Governor's honors *program, athletic schedules, community recreation schedules, day care facilities, and budgetary concerns. I was asked to make presentations for our local Rotary Club and for the parent advisory committee. At the culmination of our research, the entire school system (parents and teachers) voted on which type of calendar they preferred for next school year. Even though the modified calendar was not adopted, we learned a great deal about each other and about how each school operates under its own set of specific needs.*

As with any research endeavor, we learned more than we anticipated. We learned about areas of schools that we did not even know existed. We see each other in an entirely different light now. The experience was so positive that we are ready to investigate other issues that will ultimately impact the way we educate students in our county .I am proud to have been a part of this very important effort.

Teacher involvement is considered "essential" to the overall well-being of a school (Barth, 1999). The following is a summary of areas we found in reviewing teacher leadership inventories that links them to the three major roles we feel teacher leaders are most involved with:

- ◆ **Coaching and Mentoring Professional Relationships**
  - Designing and facilitating teacher inquiry groups
  - Building learning communities
  - Mentoring new teachers
  - Coaching peers
  - Assisting in school induction

- ◆ **Curriculum Decision Making and Instructional Improvement**
  - Choosing textbooks and instructional materials
  - Shaping the curriculum
  - Aligning the curriculum to local and national standards
  - Setting standards for student behavior and learning
  - Evaluating programs
  - Deciding how students are placed on teams and in classes

- ◆ **Involvement in School Processes and Policy Making**
  - Designing and conducting staff development and in-service programs
  - Setting promotion and retention polices

- Deciding school budgets
- Selecting new administrators
- Selecting new teachers
- Designing teacher evaluation processes and tools
- Serving as team leaders, department chairs, coordinators, committee leaders

> **Can you think of other roles your teacher leaders are involved in?**
>
> **Have you considered studying the impact on your teachers as they confront the challenges of leadership?**
>
> **How rewarding are these experiences and what problems do they encounter?**
>
> **How can you assist them in becoming better at what you have asked them to do?**

Road Blocks for Teacher Leaders

Road Block #1: Negative View of Leadership

"I'm just a teacher. If you want to talk with a leader, he's down the hall in the principal's office."

Barth, 1999

Many teachers neither view themselves as leaders, expressing openly that they do not want to serve in any administrative function, nor do they ever see themselves in a leadership position. For example, at the beginning of North Georgia College & State University's Education Specialist Program in Teacher Leadership in the summer of 2000, the majority (90 percent) of the participants (17 female and 4 male), expressed rather vehemently that they had no intentions of ever leaving their classrooms and becoming a school administrator. When asked why they had enrolled in the program for teacher leaders, one veteran teacher emphatically stated, "I've been in the classroom for more than 18 years. I doubt that there is anything more I can learn. I'm here for the money that an additional degree can help me acquire." This idea was reinforced by at least 50 percent of the group.

Glickman et al. (2001) informs us that school networks, such as the Accelerated Schools, the Effective Schools, the Comer Schools, and the League of Professional Schools, "that struggle to excel to be the definers of mainstream" serve as terrific examples but comprise less than one percent of the nation's schools (p. 465). Research studies on the Coalition of Essential Schools concluded that "different factions of teachers typically emerged within each school: the *cynics*, the *sleepy* people, the *yes-but* people, and the *teacher leaders*. Even within these reform-minded schools, …teacher leaders never constituted more than 25% of the faculty" (Barth, 1999, p .9).

Lisa's Journal

Teachers must learn to trust their ability to advance informal authority. Many of my peers do not see themselves as leaders. For the most part, teacher leadership has not been accepted. Once a teacher steps out of the classroom role to be a lead teacher or literacy coach, he or she is not viewed as one of us anymore. Until we can become more comfortable with the idea that all teachers have leadership capacity and we discover more ways teachers can comfortably lead, we will have separation and division. This lack of cohesiveness impacts on our ability to improve our schools.

What can we do to change the factions? With more than a million new teachers coming into our schools in the next few years, what can we do to change the prevailing negative school profile against teacher leaders or school leadership? Our new teachers are coming out of our preparation programs with the expectation that part of their professional responsibility is to be a contributing member of a learning community. Take a moment to review INTASC standards Nine and Ten (see Figure 7.1) for beginning teachers and the specific indicators addressed in each standard. How will you capitalize on this? "We can expect, if we choose, that all teachers will lead. Subject for negotiation need be only the manner in which each will take on some important responsibility for the betterment of the entire school community" (Barth, 1999, p. 43).

Does the "we" versus "them" attitude between teachers and administrators exist in your school? If so it must be confronted. The idea that administrators lead and teachers just follow is outdated and a waste of resources. Principals may need to consider why teachers seem to have such a negative view of school leadership. "Rightly or wrongly, teachers seem to extend their judgments of the principalship to leadership in general" (Barth, 1999, p. 39). What messages are we communicating about the role of the principal? What are your teachers' perceptions of what school administrators do?

Jana's Journal

School administrators cannot accomplish all the management issues they have while addressing instructional issues effectively. As teachers assume some of the instructional leadership responsibilities, administrators will be able to focus on other areas of school improvement. Unless teachers are willing to step up to the plate and assume these much needed leadership roles, school improvement goals will not be met as quickly as needed. Until teachers realize that they possess the same skills and qual-

ities of administrators, they will continue to look at all leaders within a school with skepticism.

Stephanie's Journal

In my opinion, building professional relationships within school communities is most important. In too many schools, there are negative feelings about teacher leadership...It is the administrator's responsibility to promote a learning community that values teacher input and goes beyond the lip service of shared decision making.

School leaders may need to study their work environment and begin to value and promote teacher leadership as a vehicle for school change and a way to train and sponsor future candidates for the principalship and beyond. This is not an easy task. For many school administrators sharing leadership with teachers is risky business, especially when they are held accountable for the outcomes. However, if teacher leadership is to emerge as a strong force within the school, the principal must express the desire for this to happen. As summarized in Figure 9.3., Barth (1999) outlines the characteristics of principals who have developed strong teacher leadership in their schools:

Figure 9.3. Principal Dispositions for Teacher Leadership

High Expectations	Teacher leadership is valued and established as a school improvement goal. Teacher leadership is part of the overall vision and mission of the school system (Lieberman, 1988).
Relinquish Power	Shared decision making is the norm. Staff members are involved in important matters through a systematic governing process. The principal makes a concerted effort to share power. Teachers need structure for their work. Teacher leadership must be legitimized within the school culture (SEDL, 1995)
Entrust	Teacher initiatives and decisions are clearly supported by the school administration even when challenged by other member of the school community.
Empower	Teachers are part of the process of addressing problems before and not after the principal has decided on a course of action. Teacher leaders do more than rubber stamp the actions of the principal.

Inclusive	All teachers are expected to emerge as a leader at some point. Resistance is made of identifying a select few teachers for involvement in decision making. There are skills and abilities that make leadership more effective. All teachers need access to information and training (SEDL, 1995).
Protect	Principals run interference for teacher leaders and support their initiatives, especially with peers. They model to the staff that they value and expect both leadership and followership among the staff. Principals accept blame if a school-wide effort falls short. They focus on what happened and what can be done to improve the situation rather than placing the blame on teachers.
Acknowledge	Principals are the guides on the side rather than the sages on the stage. Supportive principals recognize the teachers who have a led a school improvement project that has reaped a positive impact on the school community. "Good principals are more often hero-makers than heroes" (Barth, 1999, p. 37).

Road Block #2: Time and Support

Barth (1999) poses this question: "Why do so few teachers contribute so little beyond their classroom to the life of their schools? If it is such a good idea, why isn't everyone doing it?"(p. 18). One needs to look at the work conditions within the school to answer this question. Most teachers just feel overwhelmed at the current job requirements and therefore choose not to take on any additional responsibilities.

The prevailing notion of doing more with less or "working longer and harder" seems to dominate the educational scene (Donaldson, 1993). We continue to ask teachers to take on more roles and responsibilities without modifying the organizational structure to support them in these tasks. As a result we burn out those teachers who lead or force them to choose between full time teaching and any teacher leader role.

> What can you do to create schedules and work loads that will support the teacher leaders in your school?
>
> What incentives do you have to attract teachers to leadership roles and how can you reward and recognize their work?

Road Block #3: Lack of Training

Teachers who lead take on the role and responsibilities because they see a need and take action. They truly want to make a difference. However, as you can see in the excerpts you just read, the roles and tasks teacher leaders have embraced may require additional knowledge and skills such as political savvy, use of expert power and influence, interpersonal relationships, communication skills, groups dynamics, presentation skills, organizational skills, data collection and analysis skills, and coaching and mentoring skills (Lieberman, Saxl, & Miles, 1988).

According to Gehrke (1991), a major characteristic of teacher leaders is that they take on these responsibilities while teaching full- or part-time, and they learn the role by just doing it. A more systematic approach to developing teacher leaders is needed as well as more empirical evidence of the actual effectiveness of the programs designed to develop these leadership skills.

> **What staff development support can you provide to help develop your teacher leaders?**
>
> **What message will these support programs communicate about teacher leadership?**

The profession as a whole is trying to promote the cause of teacher leadership. Several colleges and universities have developed graduate-level training programs for teachers who want be involved in teacher leadership without becoming school administrators. Such programs attempt to validate and recognize the need for teacher leadership in schools. The goal of these programs is "to prepare graduates to return to their schools—*as teachers and as leaders*—prepared to strengthen relationships within their communities and promote quality change in their schools" (McCay, Flora, Hamilton, & Riley, 2001, p. 141). The degree to which this happens will be the ultimate benchmark measure of the success of these programs. Likewise, school systems need to encourage and support those teachers who desire to increase their knowledge and skills in this aspect of their professional development.

Gary's Journal

As teacher leadership advancements are made, many educators who are looking for the next step in their career may get to "have their cake and eat it too." As traditional leaders begin to ask for and willing accept help from teachers leaders, a new sense of fulfillment comes back to those teachers who have reached a plateau in their teaching career and are seeking new challenges. That challenge may mean stepping out of the classroom to take an administrative role; however, it might well just mean taking on one of the new and exciting roles offered as mentors to freshmen colleagues, serving on a local school council or any other possibility that presents itself as the idea of teacher leadership is expanded. It is an exciting time to be in education.

Beth's Journal

I can definitely see the need for more formalized training for teachers who are placed in leadership roles. Even if you are aware of all the NBPTS standards, simply knowing them is quiet different than understanding how to motivate your colleagues under your management to teach to such standards....I have been a department head in my grade level for two years. I wish I had more training to better equip me with the skills to help teachers, especially those who have serious problems and lack the motivation to improve their performance.

Barbara's Journal

Teachers must be included in the discussion about their roles as leaders. New working relationships must be created between teacher leaders and administrators. The teachers have to feel supported and understood by the principal. Without this support, there cannot be a lasting positive change for the teacher leader. Most of all teacher leaders need to be properly prepared for the leadership roles they are frequently thrown into.

Benefits of Teacher Leadership

The most important benefit of nurturing teacher leadership is the impact on the professional learning community. When teachers feel that their work is valued and that they are making a difference in their classrooms and schools, student achievement is the gain. Studies have shown that the knowledge and skills of teachers increase significantly as a result of involvement in leadership roles (Porter, 1987; Lieberman et al., 1988).

By expanding the role of experienced teachers, schools tap into a tremendous source of energy, commitment, and caring. Along with enhanced intellectual and professional growth, teacher leaders report better working relationships with their colleagues and a reduction in professional isolation as they interact in situations outside the classroom. Overall these new roles tend to increase teacher self-confidence and promote stronger commitments teaching. The force is there and it needs to be with us.

Let's revisit the teacher who expressed the idea that after 18 years in the classroom there was nothing else to learn. The following excerpt was written as she concluded her education specialist program in teacher leadership.

Written Commentary Excerpt

Curriculum Decision Making Internship—Summer 2001

In my efforts to demonstrate growth in knowledge and skills in my pursuit of standards related to this internship, I have worked diligently to meet and even exceed the requirements as outlined in each performance indicator. It has been my purpose to exhibit quality teacher leadership skills as I have worked collaboratively with my on-site mentor and other administrators. I feel I have successfully met my goals and I engaged in a variety of opportunities that have benefited all faculty, staff, and students in my school, as well as other faculty within the school system. This has been a thoroughly challenging, yet rewarding experience for me. I have gained considerable insight into school administration and the knowledge and skills needed to be an effective school leader.

Indicator I: Demonstrates the ability to use information sources, data collection and data analysis to inform decision making about curriculum changes.

"Schools that analyze and utilize information about their school communities make better decisions about not only what to change, but how to institutionalize systemic change. Schools that understand the needs of their clientele—the students—are more successful in implementing changes and remain more focused during implementation" (Bernhardt, 1998). I have worked extensively to evaluate the effectiveness of _____ County Elementary School's Extended Year Program (EYP). This program was funded by the Georgia Department of Education as a result of the mandates of House Bill 1187. Identified at-risk students in grades kindergarten through fifth grade, participated in the program from January 2001 until June 2001. In order to determine what, if any, impact the program had on student learning, I engaged in a data-gathering task that involved the collection of Basic Literary Test scores, STAR Math and STAR Reading scores (from the Learning Renaissance program adopted by the school), and 2000–2001 report card grades in the areas of reading and math for each student who participated in the program.

I will also be gathering attendance data as soon as school resumes in the fall. I also constructed surveys for parents of participating students, EYP students, and regular classroom teacher to assess perceived effectiveness of the program, as well as opportunities to make suggestions for improvements. After all the data was gathered, I compiled the data into graphs that reflected each student's progress according to grade-level and type of data. Survey responses were also graphed. I attached accompanying summaries of survey feedback with the graphs. At this time, there is still some data that is missing, due to teacher absences at the end of the school year. I made a comprehensive list of each missing piece of data so that I can look it up in each student's permanent folder.

Upon the completion of this phase of the evaluation, I met with my principal to review the results thus far. Once all the missing data has been retrieved, we will make a formal decision as to what changes will take place in the program next year. I have compiled all results into a notebook for him that he will use to compare a similar evaluation for the same program for the 2001–2002 school year.

It is only through careful evaluation of meaningful data that programs such as these can be assessed. The state did not mandate that a formal evaluation of this program take place; however, our administrators felt that if so much time, money, and instruction would be taking place, it was our responsibility as educators to determine what impact we were having on student achievement, and what improvements we could make to enhance the program for the future. I have been asked to present the findings of the evaluation of the Extended Year Program to our teachers during a faculty meeting or grade chair meetings.

I believe I have gained valuable knowledge in the essentials skills of data collection and data analysis for the purpose of making curriculum changes, specifically, the continuation of EYP. I feel the knowledge I gained in my Systematic Program Development and Evaluation course at NGCSU greatly assisted me as I strive to compile a factual, accurate, and in-depth report that will serve to guide the direction of EYP at my school. The analysis of this data will link student information together with program outcome to allow better understanding of the program as it relates to school success.

Through this excerpt we can see that our new teacher leader seems to now (a) value collaboration with colleagues and includes administrators in this process; (b) accept responsibility for curriculum improvement and data collection to support decisions and recommendations; (c) attach importance to new knowledge and skills; (d) embrace the opportunity to share results of her work with her peers; and (e) find her new experiences both challenging and rewarding.

At least for this veteran teacher, the involvement in teacher leadership development tasks and roles has provided new insight into her personal and professional capabilities and given her options for continued career growth. At the conclusion of the program, this 18-year veteran teacher continued her development by achieving NBPTS certification and pursuing her Educational Leadership Certificate. She still desires to remain in the classroom but wants to keep her options open should she decide to accept a more formal school leadership role. At least now she considers the possibility.

Career Map 9.2.
Teacher Leadership Perception Profile

Figure 9.4 presents an instrument designed to assess the inclination of teachers to move into the Teacher Leadership Career Stage. Consider sharing this instrument and asking your teachers to respond. Compile the data to determine who is ready to move into teacher leadership roles and how you might begin to develop teacher leaders in your school.

Figure 9.4. Teacher Leadership Perception Profile Inventory

Directions: Respond to the following statements in terms of how strongly you agree or disagree.

1. Strongly Disagree (SD)
2. Disagree (D)
3. Neutral/No Opinion (N)
4. Agree (A)
5. Strongly Agree (SA)

	SD1	D2	N3	A4	SA5
Curriculum Decision Making and Instructional Improvement					
• I have expert knowledge, skills, and information in my content/curriculum area that helps all students to be successful.					
• I have a clear understanding of the scope and sequence of my curriculum and its correlation to national/state standards.					
• I should have input into curriculum development that affects my students and the school.					
• I value time spent working with colleagues on curriculum and instruction.					
• I would be willing to give my time to participate in making decisions about such things as textbook adoption, budget allocation of resources, , and/or instructional organization of the school day.					
• Teachers should decide on how students might be grouped and assigned to teams and classes.					
• Teachers should be actively involved in action research in their content area in order to keep current and model best practices over their teaching career.					
• I have ongoing/critical thinking conversations with my peers about ways to improve curriculum and instruction for my students and for all students.					
Multiply each check in a column by the number at the top of each column. Now add across for the section total and place in the box below.					
Curriculum and Decision Making Total					

	SD1	D2	N3	A4	SA5
Coaching and Mentoring Professional Relationships					
• I think it is important for teachers to share their expertise with colleagues.					
• I would be willing to spend time developing my expert thinking skills on matters related to teaching and learning with my colleagues.					
• I would be willing to help a colleague who is having difficulty with his/her teaching or assignments.					
• New teachers need to have mentors who are willing to help beginners improve their practice.					
• I would be willing to be trained as teacher mentor.					
• I seek to positively influence and support my colleagues in meetings or projects at my school.					
• I would be willing to design and conduct staff development workshops for my peers in areas of school need/interest based on my expertise.					
• I have expert teaching skills and would be willing to model/share and/or demonstrate these skills.					
• I would feel comfortable observing the teaching performance of my peers and helping them to reflect on their performance.					
• I view myself as a reflective practitioner who continually sets professional goals and monitors my own teaching performance.					
Multiply each check in a column by the number at the top of each column. Then add across for the section total and place in the box below.					
Coaching and Mentoring Professional Relationships Total					

	SD 1	D 2	N 3	A 4	SA 5
Involvement in School Processes and Policy Making					
• All teachers need to be involved in the governance of the school.					
• My principal/leadership team values the input/ leadership initiatives of teachers.					
• Teachers working collaboratively should be able to influence practice and policy-making in their schools.					
• Induction and mentoring of new teachers is part of my responsibility as a professional teacher.					
• Schools should seek to become authentic professional learning communities.					
• I feel I am a productive group member when working with colleagues.					
• Teachers need to be active agents in their own professional development and career advancement based on clear standards and benchmarks.					
Multiply each check in a column by the number at the top of each column. Add across for the section total and place in the box below.					
Involvement in School Processes and Policy Making Total					

	SD 1	D 2	N 3	A 4	SA 5
Professional Self-Esteem					
• Teaching is an important profession.					
• I am a respected member of the school community.					
• I might consider becoming a school leader in the future.					
• I work in an environment where I am valued and recognized as a professional.					
Multiply each check in a column by the number at the top of each column. Add across for the section total and place in the box below.					
Professional Self-Esteem Total					

Individual Profile of Teacher Leadership

Category	*Highest Score*	*Your Score*
Curriculum Decision Making and Instructional Improvement	40	
Coaching and Mentoring Professional Relationships	50	
School Improvement Processes and Policy Making	35	
Professional Self-Esteem	25	
Total	150	

School Profile of Teacher Leadership

Category	*Highest Score*	*Average Teacher Score*	*Percent of the Total*
Curriculum Decision Making and Instructional Improvement	40		
Coaching and Mentoring Professional Relationships	50		
School Improvement Processes and Policy Making	35		
Professional Self-Esteem	25		
Total	150		

Career Map 9.3. Summarizing Results

Once you have surveyed your staff, compile your results and analyze your staff's potential for teacher leadership. Compute the average score in each category. Determine in which areas your teachers are ready to accept leadership roles and those areas you may need to strengthen through staff development and team building. What barriers exist at your school and what can you do to develop teacher leaders?

Benchmarks and Standards

As the notion of teacher leadership expands and schools become more responsive to meeting the needs of teachers based on a defined career path, guidelines for developing teacher leaders will emerge. The national reports are clear in emphasizing the need for teachers to expand their expertise beyond the classroom into school-wide leadership roles and activities (Carnegie, 1986; Holmes, 1986). National Board Certification would certainly serve as a clear benchmark—as well as career tracking—of leadership positions held, roles, accomplishments, and impact on the professional learning community. Teacher leadership portfolios using the NBPTS standards as well as standards established for school leaders—(i.e., Interstate School Leaders Licensure Consortium Standards, ISLLC)—could be designed and implemented as prompts for professional development.

North Georgia College & State University has developed its teacher leadership program based on both state and national standards. In this program, Education Specialist candidates complete thirty hours of coursework and field-based internships (beyond the Master's Degree) centering on building knowledge, skill, and collaborative relationships within schools, and producing artifacts that meet both individual professional development goals and the needs of the school community to increase student learning and achievement.

After a year-long planning process and review of the professional literature on teacher leadership, the Education Specialist design team, comprised of education faculty and school practitioners, targeted the following issues as the core curriculum for the specialist degree in teacher leadership. (Visit NGCSU Web page—Graduate Programs for EDS Program overview).

- ◆ TCHL: 7001—Applying Systematic Learning Frameworks to Increase Student Achievement

- ◆ TCHL: 7002—Building Leadership Capacity in Schools and Communities

- ◆ TCHL: 7003—Developing Productive Work Groups for School Improvement and Innovation

♦ TCHL: 7004—Coaching and Mentoring Professional Relationships

♦ TCHL: 7005—Generating and Using Assessment and Research Data for Increasing Student Achievement

♦ TCHL: 7006—Using Inquiry-Based Methods for Curriculum Development

♦ TCHL: 7007—Planning Strategically for Systematic Program Development and Evaluation

♦ TCHL: 7008—Expanding Professional Roles in Education: Ethical and Legal Implications

♦ TCHL: 7009—NBPTS Pre-Candidate Portfolio Development

Concurrently, candidates are intensively involved with site-based mentors holding leadership certification and/or instructional supervision endorsements in designing and implementing action plans that target specific standards in each of these three areas:

1. TCHL 7901 Teacher Mentoring Internship
2. TCHL 7902 Instructional Supervision Internship
3. TCHL 7903 Curriculum Decision-Making Internship

These internships provide the culminating or capstone experiences for the Educational Specialist Degree in Teacher Leadership at NGCSU, as well as the completion of two entries required for the National Board Certification process.

The NGCSU program beginning in the summer of 2000 graduated its first cohort of twenty students (95 percent completion rate) in the summer of 2001. Four candidates opted to complete NBPTS certification while enrolled in the specialist program and three passed (75 percent). Sixty percent of the cohort progressed to complete the add-on requirements for leadership certification. Program evaluations from all stakeholders and a program review by the Southern Association of Colleges and Schools cite the following aspects as key strengths of the program:

Commendation 1: The committee commends the NGCSU faculty for the excellent design of the Ed.S program, melding both national and state standards in a coherent curriculum to prepare teacher leadership.

Commendation 2: The committee commends the faculty of the Ed.S Degree Program for excellence in instruction. There is ample evidence of careful planning of instructional activities and assignments, design and use of rubrics for evaluation of student performance, mentoring and supervision of internships and portfolio development.

◆ The faculty are commended for being flexible enough to utilize student informal feedback to adjust expectations, assignments, and teaching activities appropriately, while consistently maintaining high quality expectations and standards.

◆ Faculty and program administrators work closely together to ensure continuity and communication from course to course, semester to semester, and to appropriately involve adjunct fatuity (school leaders and NBPTS certified teachers) and other resources from the public schools in meaningful ways that benefit student learning and performances as teacher leaders.

SACS Final Report, October 2001—A copy of the entire report can be obtained from NGCSU.

Career Stage Summary: Teacher Leader

How do we go about transforming the conventional school in which all teachers lead and leadership capacity is valued and developed? According to Donaldson (1993), "the transition from traditional patterns of faculty problem solving and decision-making to more collaborative ones is fraught with difficulties….Leading collaborative change in schools means helping staffs become more productive without substantially depleting their resources." It means working smarter, not longer. As Fullean and Hargreaves (1991) note, "Building collaborative cultures involves a long-term developmental journey; there are no shortcuts."

We have asked school principals to share what they do and what they might do differently in moving toward this goal. How are principals helping their staffs to work smarter, not longer, as they involve them in teacher leadership?

From the Principal's Desk…

Because our path is never ending and takes many turns, our school cannot operate successfully with only one or two leaders, and certainly a principal cannot go it alone. Many must fill that role. I try to provide an environment in which teacher leadership grows and flourishes. The measure of a good leader is not how many followers you develop but how many leaders you develop. I feel a deep responsibility for the health and performance of our teacher leaders. I do everything within my power to help teachers who want to move on to leadership positions outside of the classroom. I have been a principal for 18 years, and, during that time, 15 teachers on my faculty have taken leadership positions in the areas of counseling, curriculum, administration and staff development. I try very hard to be a leader of leaders.

Teacher leaders are nurtured in a school environment of inquiry, trust, and empowerment. If the principal is fearful of losing control and holds firmly to the reins, teacher leadership will not flourish. Leaders will not be born. Unfortunately, many teachers have a negative view of school leadership based on the role models they have experienced and, as a result, do not wish to venture out on those waters. Schools that spawn teacher leaders view shared leadership as the best way to move the school forward on the road to continuous improvement. Let me give some specific examples of what I do to foster teacher leadership in my school:

· Teacher leadership is expected of ALL teachers, not just a few handpicked by me. Several programs, structures, and processes are in place that promote continuous improvement and produce a community of leaders at our school. Our Local School Advisory Committee meets monthly as a cohesive force in the school. Teachers serve on this important committee on a rotating basis enabling us to hear the voices of many. Our School Based Planning and Evaluation Team, which includes parents, staff, and faculty members, ensures that all programs and resources are aligned with our identified goals and objectives. Again, teachers serve on a rotating basis on this team. Our School Leadership Team is composed of representatives from every grade level and department. The membership rolls over every two to three years, enabling others to take an active leadership role. Some teachers come "kicking and screaming" to the leadership role to only discover they were "closet" leaders just needing the expectation and nudge.

· Positive Perception of Leadership. I treat my teachers with respect and trust. I try to follow the old adage: "Better to be fooled by a few than suspicious of many." I assume they are doing a good job; I assume they will take their turn at the bat as a leader; and I assume some will remain as leaders willingly. Always, they are treated with respect, which is not to say that I don't take action when needed if behavior warrants; however, always done privately and with suggestions for how to regroup and move forward.

· I portray my job in a positive tone no matter how tired and frustrated I become and no matter how late I have to stay each day to prepare for the next one. I portray my job to teachers as if I have the energy, passion, and expertise to carry it out in an effective way (when in fact many times I do not). I am reminded of Tom Hanks' role in the movie, "Saving Private Ryan." When asked by his troop subordinates why he never complained about the hardships of combat and his job, his response was, "I don't complain to you, only to my superiors." What a simple example of how a leader instills trust and respect in him as a leader by portraying himself in a positive manner. Those men under his command are left with an image of leadership that helps them make future decisions about their own leadership possibilities. In turn, I hope my teachers view leadership in a positive light through my example and are more willing to step forth themselves.

- *Coaching and Mentoring Professional Relationships.* I involve the entire faculty when new teachers join our profession, staff, or just change grade levels/subject areas. I provide the framework of support by involving our well-trained mentors as well as the other members of the grade level/department of the novice. An induction team is formed for all who need their support. I make sure the induction team members have the skills to do the job, and, if not, I provide the needed training for them. Through a local school committee recommendation, additional teachers are recommended every year to be trained as mentors. When we have a new focus, program, or initiative for our school or district, I make certain that teachers receive quality coaching from an expert (hopefully in house expert) to learn the skills needed. Mentoring and coaching is expected and valued.

- *Curriculum Decision Making and Instructional Improvement.* Recently, through a local school improvement process, we decided to redesign our curriculum to better serve our students. Out of this initiative, leaders were tapped as well as discovered. They led small groups through curriculum revision, compacting, and alignment. My job was to make sure the group leaders had the training and tools to do the job. I did all the behind-the-scenes work to make their job as leaders easier, i.e., modeling the skills myself for leaders to observe, providing all clerical support needed, providing the time needed to devote to the task. Canceling faculty meetings so time was available for the job, hiring substitutes to cover classes so leaders can work with experts in the field and learn how best to lead their groups are a few examples.

- *Involvement in School Processes and Policy Making.* Perhaps a description of the process we used that recently earned us the prestigious recognition as a Georgia School of Excellence might be the best way to describe "how we do things around here." The application process is grueling, challenging, and requires a lot of work by everyone in the school. We have applied for the award in the past with no success. Since I had completed most of the application work myself, I knew the amount of work involved and had no intention of going through that process again to no avail. Two teachers came to me and asked if we would apply this year and I gave them the response I just described. Their response was, "We think we are a school of excellence and deserve that recognition. Would you agree for us to complete the application that would lead to that end?" I agreed, although reluctantly, knowing how much work was ahead for all of us and how much work I must do to empower and support the two teacher volunteers.

· The first step I took was to design a framework that I felt would enable these two teachers to accomplish their task. I announced to our faculty that I felt we truly deserved the honor, and that two teachers had sought the opportunity to lead us through the process. I met with our school leadership team to gain insights on our pending plan as well as model brainstorming techniques for them to use when working with their colleagues. The team members elicited ideas on every question in the application which immediately immersed the entire school community into the reflective process. Each grade level/department then transferred their ideas to large posters in the faculty dining room. As a result, one could walk into the staff dining room and see every question and every idea from every member of the staff. When ideas came to them while they were eating lunch, they could easily jump up and add to the posters.

· I asked each staff member to choose the question area they wished to devote more time to in the preparation of the application. The school leadership team served as chairs for each topic on the application, and, subsequently, collected all the data that had been generated on the charts making that information available to their groups. I, along with my administrative team and secretaries, pulled together all the information that each group would need and made the information readily accessible to them as they worked. A small group of writers under the leadership of our two volunteer writers began to write the report as each committee completed their recommendations. The plan was presented to our Local School Advisory Team which included staff, parents, and business partners for their input.

· Now our two volunteer lead writers went to work. I provided them with release time and secretarial help to complete their task as well as many pats on the back. I took their draft and refined it if needed. We provided a copy of the completed application for every member of the staff so they could appreciate all the hard work that all of them had done. And the waiting began! Several months later, we were notified by our state school superintendent that we had received the award. Many opportunities to celebrate the recognition came our way over the following weeks. We were recognized by our school board, newspapers, and school district publications. Always, I proclaimed that this was a schoo-wide effort and recognized our lead writers and other teacher leaders for the outstanding work they had done.

· Interesting how much richer this experience was when I tapped our teacher leadership capacity than when I did most of the work myself in the previous application process. But also noteworthy is how much I, as the building leader, had to do behind the scenes to insure that our teacher leaders were successful in their endeavors for our school. I've highlighted examples of those tasks in the above text. Hopefully, this experience, as well as many others like this one, is developing and broadening our teacher leadership base.

Being a leader of leaders is hard work!

References

Barth, R. (1999). *Teacher leader*. Providence, RI: The Rhode Island Foundation

Boyd-Dimock, V. & McGree, K. M. (1995). Leading change from the classroom: Teachers as leaders. *Issues About Change*, 4(4), Austin, TX: Southwest Educational Development Laboratory (SEDL). http://www.sedl.org/change/issues/issues44.html. Retrieved 8/21/01.

Carnegie Forum on Education and the Economy. (1986). *A nation prepared: Teachers for the 21st century*. New York: Carnegie Forum on Education and the Economy.

Donaldson, G. (1993). Working smarter together. *Educational Leadership, 51*(2).

Fullan, M., & Hargreaves, A. (1991). *What's worth fighting for? Working together for your school*. Andover, MA: Regional Laboratory of the Northeast and Islands.

Gehrke, N. (1991). *Developing teachers' leadership skills*. (ERIC Document Reproduction Service No: ED33061)

The Holmes Group (1986). *Tomorrow's teachers*. East Lansing, MI: Author.

Katzenmeyer, M., & Moller, G. (2000). *Awakening the sleeping giant*. Thousand Oaks, CA: Corwin Press.

Lieberman, A., Saxl, E., & Miles, M. (1988). Teacher leadership: Ideology and practice. In A. Lieberman (Ed.), *Building a professional culture in schools*. New York: Teachers College Press.

Livingston, C. (1992). Teacher leadership for restructured schools. In C. Livingston (Ed.), *Teachers as leaders: Evolving roles*. NEA School Restructuring Series. Washington, DC: National Educational Association.

McCay, L., Flora, J., Hamilton, A., & Riley, J. (2001, Spring). Reforming schools through teacher leadership: A program for classroom teachers as agents of change. *Educational Horizons*, 135–141.

McLaughlin, M., & Mei-ling, Y. (1988). In A. Lieberman (Ed.), *Building a professional culture in schools*. New York: Teachers College Press.

O'Conner, K., & Boles, K. (1992). *Assessing the needs of teacher leaders in Massachusetts*. Paper presented at the annual meeting of the American Educational Research Association, San Francisco.

Pellicer, L. O., & Anderson, L. W. (1995). *Handbook for teacher leaders*. Thousand Oaks, CA: Corwin Press.

Porter, A. (1986) Teacher collaboration: New partnerships to attract old problems. *Kappan, 69*(2).

Sherrill, J. (1999). Preparing teachers for leadership roles in the 21st century. *Theory into Practice, 38*(1) 56–62.

Troen, V., & Boles, K. (1992, April). *Leadership from the classroom: Women teachers as a key to school reform*. Paper presented at the annual meeting of the American Educational Research Association, San Francisco.

Wasley, P.A. (1991). *Teachers who lead: The rhetoric of reform and the realities of practice*. New York: Teachers College Press.

Wilson, M. (1993). The search for teacher leaders. *Educational Leadership, 50*(6).

Teacher Leadership: Resources and Internet Tools

http://www.nsdc.org
National Staff Development Council

     Library Resources—*When Teachers Lead*

http://www.edweek.org
Education Week on the Web—*Leadership for Student Learning: Redefining the Teacher as Leader*

     School Leadership for the 21st Century Initiative

     April 2001: A Report of the Task Force on Teacher Leadership
     http://www.edweek.org/ew/ewstory.cfm?slug=32teach.h20

http://www.nsba.org
National School Boards Association

     Education Leadership Toolkit

     http://www.nsba.org/sbot/toolkit/index.html

Career
Stage Four:
Teacher Steward

10

Professional Continuity and Commitment

*One man has enthusiasm for 30 minutes, another
for 30 days, but it is the man who has it for 30 years
who makes a success of his life.*

> Edward Butler, American Scientist (NASSP, Great
> Quotations, 1985)

Defining the Teacher Steward Career Stage

In this career framework, educators who have achieved the skills and benchmarks as a Teacher Specialist and Teacher Leader make the decision to reach another level of their career development by selecting paths that take them to service levels within the profession. As a Teacher Steward, these educators are very concerned with making a contribution to the next generation of teachers, schools, and students. Within this context, we define a Teacher Steward as a teacher who may: (a) continue full-time teaching but assumes additional roles that support teaching and learning; (b) leave full-time teaching but takes on the challenge of sustained contributions to the profession in formal leadership roles at the school or central office level; or (c) formally retire from the profession but remains active in a particular role that still motivates him or her to continue service to the profession.

Case Story #1

Jean has been a high school English teacher for more than 25 years. During that time, she acquired her doctorate in curriculum and instruction, has written several articles in her content area, and has taken a special interest in guiding skills, Jean volunteered to be trained as a mentor when the system began offering staff development courses through the local university. Jean expanded her mentorship by accepting student teachers from teacher preparation institutions and working with university faculty in developing better ways to induct new teachers into the profession.

As a result of Jean's modeling, demonstration, and coaching of expert teaching skills in her content area, students placed with Jean also showed high levels of content mastery and application. Jean was asked by the teacher education faculty to serve as a part-time adjunct faculty member and teach courses related to her teaching field during evening and Saturday classes whenever she could fit these classes into her teaching schedule. Jean believes that training teachers for the profession is very important, and she uses her current teaching situation as a lab for both undergraduate and graduate classes.

Teacher Education

If pre-service teacher education is to strengthen its mission of preparing the nation's teachers, those who have teaching expertise and experience in the content fields need to enter the playing field. Through the use of clinical professors, part-time adjunct instructors, co-teaching with cooperating teachers and trained mentors, and partnership in professional development schools, educators in K–12 schools can play a very important role in preparing the next generation of teachers.

This career opportunity brings back into the profession the accumulated teaching experiences of successful expert teachers who have sustained productive years in classrooms and provides pre-service teachers with authentic role models. Schools of Education need to seek out these talented teachers and those who achieve NBPTS certification and need to provide avenues for incorporating these teachers' contributions. Competent teachers with more than 20 years of teaching notched on their belt seeking to make a contribution in teacher preparation should be encouraged by teacher education institutions and their school systems to pursue advanced degrees that would qualify them for positions in higher education.

Case Story #2

Margo has been a middle school science teacher for 10 years. During that time, she has acquired National Board Certification and her education specialist degree in teacher leadership. Margo desires to help schools become professional learning communities. Her involvement in teacher leadership activities and the NBPTS process has expanded her ideas of school leadership and even the possibility of a future role as a principal.

When the opportunity arose at her school for an additional assistant principal, the principal asked Margo to apply. However, because Margo had young children at home, she felt she could not take on a full-time administrative position. Margo asked the principal if the administrative assignment could be split between two teacher leaders who wanted to move into school leadership but also wanted to remain in the classroom. The principal agreed and in the process kept two talented teachers in the classroom and also acquired two assistant principals. Margo believes that teachers in a school are the driving force in transforming schools into learning communities. She hopes to convince her colleagues of their abilities as teacher leaders.

Case Story #3

Rachel has been an elementary school teacher and special education resource teacher for more than 15 years. During this time, she completed her education specialist degree and is currently seeking National Board certification. Rachel views herself as a lifelong learner and believes that professional development is essential to maintaining high levels of teaching and learning in schools. To this end, as the result of her interest in adult learning and development, she has designed and conducted numerous staff development programs at her school and for the school system. When the position of staff development coordinator came up at her school, Rachel applied and was strongly recommended by her principal and peers for this career change based on her expertise and credibility with adult learners. As the coordinator for staff development, Rachel hopes to help all teachers achieve their potential as master teachers in the profession. She believes that there are many teachers who have exceptional expertise and that this expertise needs to be cultivated and used to help other teachers within their schools.

School Leadership

If schools are to develop into authentic teaching learning communities, more attention needs to be directed to those individuals who move into building-level and central office positions. We think teachers who have confirmed and validated their instructional competence in the Specialist Stage and tested and honed their collaborative leadership skills in the Teacher Leader Stage are prime candidates for these necessary roles. The research is clear on this point: The principal is the key player in setting the context for the teaching and learning climate in every school.

However, "young (aspiring) principals are not a common sight in the nation's schools" and experts in the field are concerned that the void rapidly developing by retiring school leaders is not being filled (Stricherz, 2001, p. 6). The first wave of baby-boomer principals are now eligible to retire in many states, but, based on recent statistics, "baby busters" born after 1964 have stepped up to school leadership positions in certain areas. According to figures compiled by the National Association of Elementary School Principals (NAESP), the percentage nationally of K–8 principals younger than 35 dropped from almost 5 percent of all school leaders in 1988 to just 1.3 percent in 1998. NAESP estimates that 40 percent of the nation's total of 93, 000 principals of K–12 schools will need to be replaced by 2006, mostly as a result of retirements.

The role of the principal is complicated and requires high levels of skill in such areas as instructional leadership and supervision, data collection to document student learning, school-community collaboration, and organizational oversight to meet school goals and standards. Paul Houston, the executive director of the American Association of School Administrators, comments that young professionals are not being actively recruited for leadership positions. Jon Schnur, chief executive officer of New Leaders for New Schools, asserts that the country lacks a "systematic approach to developing these people" (Stricherz, 2001).

Overall, the job is not viewed in a positive light. Accountability demands and higher standards are deterring teachers and assistant principals from moving into the ranks of the principalship. According to Jill Levy, president of the Council of Supervisors and administrators in New York, "the demands of the academic standards movement and the bureaucracy of large districts make it hard for young school leaders to be hired….The job is so complicated, and it's such an accountable position, that young principals, teachers, and assistant principals aren't feeling prepared to enter the ranks of principals" (Stricherz, 2001, p. 7).

Shortages of principals in areas where districts are often desperate to hire school leaders have led to the hiring of individuals with less teaching and administrative experience. Some leadership preparation programs have shortened the length and scope of their programs to graduate program completers after 10 months instead of the two to three years required by most programs.

We believe teacher education programs and school systems can begin to develop and train a large pool of prospective school leaders from the teacher leadership ranks. In NGCSU's Education Specialist Program, teacher leaders are encouraged and invited to pursue school leadership positions through the add-on certification program in Educational Leadership. These individuals, through a year-long internship, also work with their current school principal and leadership team on administrative projects and activities that help to give them a very clear snapshot of the complexities of the job and the opportunity to test their commitment in a career path of service in developing a productive school and vibrant school community.

School systems can build on the needs of teacher leaders to have more ownership and responsibility in the school improvement process by utilizing these individuals in ways that move the school forward and by tapping those individuals who are willing to continue their training and move into school administration.

The key to this happening is how teacher leadership is viewed and how teacher leaders are developed and inducted into the more formal roles of school leadership. We have seen negative views of school leadership shift as teacher leaders work side by side with competent, collaborative, and caring principals. The notion that "I can do this work" begins to evolve, and many teacher leaders become proactive supporters of their leaders as they begin to get the bigger picture of what a school principal or central office administrator thinks, does, and believes is important in leading a school or school system.

Matt's Journal

According to Glickman (1998, p. 343) as groups work together, the leader needs to practice skills that enable the group to become more cohesive, responsible and autonomous. The leader must do the basic tasks such as preparing and distributing an agenda prior to the meeting, keeping the meeting running on time, and establishing ground rules for the meeting. The effective leader must also understand the various group roles and know how to deal with dysfunctional group members.

As I have observed and worked with my building administrator, I have learned that organization and enthusiasm are two keys to success when trying to motivate people. Prior planning and clear goal setting for faculty and committee meetings models effective use of time and shows respect for teachers' time. Planning and scheduling the work of teachers is especially important when new work groups are initiated. By observing my principal, I have realized the importance of effective work groups and managing conflict as soon as it emerges. I have learned to deal with conflict by observing and applying the process of conflict resolution in my school.

Christie's Journal

Collaboration is defined as working jointly with others in an intellectual endeavor, according to the American Heritage Dictionary. Glickman (1998) points out that if ideas are judged on the basis of their merits and not on the power of the individual, then collaboration is at work. Whether one is a teacher, supervisor, student, or parent, collaboration means each individual in the group has the right to have his or her ideas judged on the basis of their merit and credibility toward solving a problem. Ideas should not be judged on the fact that some people in the group have more power than others....My principal models this collaborative approach. She involves all group members in the discussion and walks the talk of shared decision making.

Bill's Journal

If schools are to be successful, supervision must respond to teachers as changing adults. This point is made even clearer by Evans in his book, The Human Side of School Change, when he talks about the teaching force being made up mainly of people in middle age and in mid-to-late career. He talks about the mid-life teacher as being wiser, calmer, and having a deeper understanding of others. He also contends that the mid-career teacher begins to focus more on issues outside of school, unlike the teacher who is focused on mastering the skill of teaching. The mid-career teacher has become a master of the skill. Teaching is not as challenging as it used to be. Mid-career teachers see change as a fine-tuning of skills rather than sweeping innovation as a new teacher may see it.

For a supervisor to effect change when working with the middle-age teacher who is in mid-to-late career, he or she has to us different approaches than ones used with a beginning teacher. I believe that supervisors must be aware of the developmental stages of the adult leaner in order to attain high levels of personal and professional development.

Staff development in my school system is not viewed in any systematic way. Teachers are basically grouped as a whole and are not viewed developmentally either by age, career stages, or expertise. As I have worked with the staff development director in our system, we have discussed staff development approaches that consider the characteristics of adult learners suggested in the professional literature. Together, we are drafting a proposal that would begin to address research-based professional development principles outlined by the National Partnership for Excellence and Accountability in Teaching (http://www.npeat.org).

Case Story #4

Tom, age 60, has been a retired high school math teacher for five years and has been recognized as *Teacher of the Year* several times in his teaching career. He has spent the last three years working part-time in the school system helping high school dropouts get their equivalency diploma. Tom knows that there are students who get lost in the cracks of large high schools, and he wanted to be there when they came back to complete their high school education. Tom also works with the community school director in designing adult education programs to meet the educational needs of the community. He also serves as a volunteer in the community's Literacy Program and occasionally will take on a short-term substitute position to help the local high school, when full time staff members need health or emergency leaves.

Life After Retirement

Teachers and administrators who retire are probably the most neglected group in the teaching career cycle. In this stage, teachers who are approaching retirement and those who have formally retired are probably the largest group of teachers in the work force. These are the baby boomers, ranging in age from 45 to 55, and their numbers are significant. According to Steffey et al. (2000), veteran teachers who retire have been significantly underutilized as a valuable resource for public schools.

What comes to mind when you think of the term retirement? Reward? Release? Renewal? What images do you have of teachers and administrators who are 55 and over? Burned out? Withdrawn? Asset? Our American culture is very much youth-oriented. What biases do you hold about age and the quality of work from those educators who are reaching senior status? More important, what perceptions/attitudes do these individuals have about remaining active and involved in their profession? What can we do to capitalize on their years of service and continue to build on their expertise to help schools, teachers, and students?

Bridging the Gaps

The teachers cited above in the case stories have entered the Teacher Steward Career Stage in various ways. Having invested many years in the profession, achieving high levels of expertise and wisdom, and perhaps serving as teacher leaders and school administrators, these teachers are clearly unique. The accomplished teacher and administrator possess several important qualities. First, they have firsthand knowledge and skill of specific job roles; second, they usually have more than 20 years of accumulated craft knowledge of their school and or school system, and, third, they have the desire to continue making a significant contribution to the profession. These individuals provide threads of continuity within the profession and help to transmit and transform our professional culture. Figure 10.1 revisits this career stage and reviews the career retention risks inherent to it.

Figure 10.1. Teacher Steward: Adult Development Needs and Retention Risks

Career Stage	Adult Development Needs	Career Retention Risks
Teacher Steward 45 to 65	• Biological capabilities begin to decline • Senior status in unique worlds and the desire to be responsible not only for own work but also for the development of the current generation of young adults who will soon follow • Key developmental task is the process of individuation. The adult becomes more compassionate, more reflective, more judicious, less ruled by inner conflicts and external demands • Acceptance of life and affiliations • Focus on completing important activities	• Early retirement results from lack of desire to give back to profession • Inability to capitalize on the expertise of the practitioner and redirect where needed in the system • Outdated staffing patterns that would meet needs of mature teachers who wish to teach part-time and/or assist with developing curriculum and mentoring new teachers

What thoughts do you have about this career stage?

How can we go about capitalizing on this career stage and promoting and retaining those who desire to make a difference?

Career Stage Summary: Teacher Steward

From the Principal's Desk...

As outstanding teachers either leave for career changes or retire and "fade away into the sunset," our school falters, stumbles for a period; our light dims ever so slightly, and our teacher retention rate drops temporarily. Our teacher leaders have moved on, and we miss them. We miss their leadership, their expert knowledge, their exemplary teaching skills, and their role model for us all. What a void! As a principal, I have viewed this event as a rite of passage inevitable for a maturing faculty, chalked it off to "that's just the way it is," and moved on to try to somehow rebound with their replacements. The retiree didn't look back nor did I. We all moved on.

Oh, how I overlooked an untapped resource for our profession! Do we have to let them go? Do they have to go? Many of our teachers complete 25 to 30-plus years of teaching, yet they are still physically and mentally vital, still passionate about their chosen profession, still want to contribute; yet we bid them adieu. Is there something I could do to continue to enable us to benefit from their talents while they enjoyed more time for friends and family, a slower pace, and a reduction of responsibility? My personal brainstorming produced the following possibilities for our potential retirees:

- Part-time teacher—Two or three days a week in a position that doesn't require full time teacher, i.e., remedial education, special education, gifted education, advanced placement courses, critical field courses (science, math, etc.).
- Job share—Share position with another teacher with a need for a creative schedule (maybe teacher with young children or even another retiree).
- Instructor for staff development in area(s) of expertise.
- Mentor for beginning teachers.
- Supervisor of beginning teachers for a college/university.
- Consultant for school/district projects and committees.
- Writer of professional articles/books.
- Substitute: teacher, department chair, administrator, curriculum coordinator.

At times, I have tried to convince retired teachers to come back in some of the above capacities. And usually the answer is "no." But why is that? I think our school provides a very positive work environment for anyone, so why not come back in some reduced way? My speculations generate a couple of possibilities as explanations:

1. Once retiring teachers leave, they move onto a life that they have been planning for a long time because they thought there were no viable options left for them in a semi-retirement mode. They are unable and/or unwilling to alter those plans after the fact.

2. We, as leaders, do not inform, guide, or encourage our potential retirees regarding the possibilities available to them in the next level of the teacher career ladder while still enjoying many of the perks of retirement.

I will have to admit that every idea in this entry constitutes "Things I Wish I Had Done," for I have done none of them. It is incumbent upon all of us to open this next path of the teacher career ladder as our best and finest educators move to the next chapter in their professional lives. That level which affords them time to reflect, hone their skills, direct their energies in the professional areas they love and still have time for friends, family, fun, and travel. What an ideal job! Let's not miss this opportunity for our colleagues, for ourselves, and for our profession.

What I Will Do Differently in the Future For Our Teacher Leaders Before They Reach Retirement Age:

· Encourage them to explore all possibilities for professional contributions well before they reach retirement, including advanced degrees in areas of interest.
· Provide opportunities for our expert teachers to develop and conduct staff development courses for our faculty/district.
· Encourage attendance at conferences/seminars on Effective Presentation Skills and Technology Proficiency.
· Recommend enrollment in teacher mentoring courses.
· Assign them to mentor beginning teachers.
· Encourage and celebrate their professional writing and publications.
· Include some of these opportunities in their individual growth plan over time so when retirement opportunities arrive, they are ready to go!

We often write off potential retirees for opportunities such as these, feeling they are not good investments of money and training since they will soon be gone. We don't invest in them so naturally they don't invest in us in their later years. We all need a paradigm shift regarding our vintage teacher leaders. I'm ready!

References

Steffey, B. E., Wolfe, M. P., Pasch, S. H., and Enz, B. J. (Eds.). (2000). *Life cycle of the career teacher.* Thousand Oaks, CA: Corwin Press

Stricherz, M. (2001, October 24). Despite retirements, 'baby busters' scarce in principals' positions. *Education Week,* p. 6.

Teacher Steward: Resources and Internet Tools

http://www.npeat.org
National Partnership for Excellence and Accountability in Teaching

> http://www.npeat.org/public_html/public_html/public_html/strand2/pdprin.pdf

> *Professional Development Research Principles*

> NPEAT is a voluntary association of 29 national organizations and several major research universities dedicated to research-based

action that results in teaching excellence to raise student performance. This site provides direct links to these associations and their work in three key areas:

1. Teacher Education and Recruitment
2. Induction and Professional Development
3. Standards and Assessment

http://www.ed.gov
U.S. Department of Education

Model Professional Development Programs

Quoted form the Web site:

To be recognized, schools and districts demonstrate that their professional development programs result in improved teacher effectiveness and student learning and are consistent with a set of principles for professional development that are based on the best available research and exemplary practice. Winners must have demonstrated that student achievement data has increased over three years....Developing the skills of teachers and principals plays a critical role in school improvement. **High-quality programs include rigorous subject content, effective teaching strategies and school- and district-based supports that ensure the career-long development of teachers.**